Which Church?

which
CHURCH?

How to identify a biblical church

Edited by Robert Strivens

EVANGELICAL PRESS

Evangelical Press
Faverdale North Industrial Estate, Darlington, DL3 0PH England
email: sales@evangelicalpress.org

Evangelical Press USA
PO Box 825, Webster, NY 14580 USA
email: usa.sales@evangelicalpress.org

www.evangelicalpress.org

First published 2007

Printed in the United Kingdom

British Library Cataloguing in Publication Data available

ISBN-13: 978 085234 6686   *ISBN-10: 0852346689*

Contents

Foreword (Philip Eveson)   7

1. The Freedom of the Free Churchman (Paul Cook)   9

2. The Roots of Nonconformity (Robert Oliver)   27

3. The Nonconformist Minister (Stuart Olyott)   47

4. Nonconformist Preaching (Geoffrey Thomas)   73
   Dr Lloyd-Jones Memorial Lecture

5. The Decline of Nonconformity (Kenneth Brownell)   103

6. Nonconformist Anglicans? (Melvin Tinker)   127

7. The Future of Nonconformity (Mark Johnston)   139

Epilogue (Robert Strivens)   153

Notes   159

Foreword

For many evangelicals, questions of church government and structure are of no significance. In deciding what church to attend, their only questions relate to the content of the preaching and the style of worship. If the sermons are biblical and the singing acceptable, why should we quibble over the denomination or grouping to which the church happens to belong?

But the Bible is a demanding book, and it is a characteristic of the Nonconformist conscience that it cannot rest satisfied with a mere obedience in part. Every consistent evangelical must seek to obey *all* of Scripture, so far as he understands it, because obedience to *all* of Scripture is what Christ commands. The Nonconformist believes that the Bible has something very definite to say about how a local church is to be organized and governed, and about how it is to relate to other local churches. We believe that the pattern laid down in the New Testament on these matters is not a matter of indifference which may be neglected. And so, though of course the content of the preaching and worship is vital, the question of the government and inter-church relations of the churches we attend are matters which we cannot simply ignore.

To examine these issues, the John Owen Centre for Theological Study organized a conference entitled 'Where have all the Nonconformists gone?' which took place on 20 and 21 September 2004. These are the papers delivered on that occasion. Robert Oliver presents a historical overview of Nonconformity, Ken Brownell focuses on the nineteenth-century experience of a prominent Nonconformist chapel in Birmingham, Paul Cook expounds the glorious liberty of the Free Churchman, Stuart

Olyott looks at the biblical basis of the Nonconformist view of the pastoral ministry, Mark Johnston gives us a glimpse of the future of Nonconformity, Geoff Thomas, in the Lloyd-Jones Memorial Lecture, inspires us to hear and emulate the best Nonconformist preaching, and Melvin Tinker argues the case for Nonconformist Anglicanism. All have in common an overriding desire to be biblical in the way in which we organize ourselves and operate as local bodies of believers.

The apostle Paul describes the church as 'the pillar and ground of the truth' (1 Tim. 3:15). May these papers help us to think through more clearly and biblically what the New Testament has to say about the shape and structure of that vital body, and so return to a more vigorous biblical Nonconformity, to the glory of the Lord of the church, Jesus Christ.

Philip Eveson
London Theological Seminary

Chapter 1

The Freedom of the Free Churchman

Paul E. G. Cook

Introduction and definitions

I was asked to prepare a paper on the subject of 'The Biblical Basis of the Freedom of the Church', or some title like that, and to look at the subject in the light of modern state interference, etc., as well as in the past. Recovering from the shock, I reflected for a while and thought that the title 'The Freedom of the Free Churchman' just about covered the assignment. This also gives me the opportunity to rove somewhat randomly over the whole field of Nonconformity without trespassing upon the subjects covered by the other papers.

The terms 'Free Church' and 'Free Churchman' are the twentieth-century versions of the more usual late nineteenth-century designation 'Nonconformist', a term dating back to Elizabeth I's reign and used of those inside the Established Church who would not conform to some of the practices prescribed by the 1559 Prayer Book.[1] Strictly speaking, Nonconformity is a form of behaviour defined by law and exists where there are those who refuse to submit to restrictive legislation. Remove the restriction, and Nonconformity ceases to exist. In this sense, the sixteenth-century Separatists on the one hand and Bishop John Hooper and others of like conviction within the Established Church on the other hand were all Nonconformists.

We usually refer to the early seventeenth-century Baptists and Congregationalists as 'Dissenters'. However, the term

'Dissenter' can legitimately be used of those within the Church of England at that time who were dissatisfied with the half-reformed hybrid produced by the Elizabethan Settlement, and could therefore include those of Presbyterian and Congregational conviction, many of whom sought refuge in the 1620s and 1630s in the New World. But the term 'Dissenter' did not come into use until after the Glorious Revolution of 1688 and only became general as a description of non-Episcopal congregations in the early eighteenth century. These Baptist, Congregational and Presbyterian churches have been designated the 'Old Dissent', and were little influenced by the eighteenth-century Evangelical Revival. The churches which came into being as a result of the revival have been described as the 'New Dissent'. Moving into the nineteenth century, the most usual term to describe all these Nonconformists was 'Dissenters' and this included the various Methodist groupings.

The twentieth-century term 'Free Church' suggests that the struggle for the liberty of worship and conscience has been won. Apart from the liabilities of prejudice and patronage imposed by the existence of the Established Church, that is substantially the situation. The Nonconformist is now 'free', though he is still excluded from a number of privileges, and in certain situations is expected to conform to the religion of the Establishment.

The modern Nonconformist, however, is now confident enough to display outside his place of worship such signs as 'Free Church' and 'Evangelical Free Church', though whether the worshippers know what the word signifies is open to question. Ask them, and you will get an amazing range of answers, and as for the passer-by, he frequently thinks — with better historical sense than he might imagine — that the seating is free, while others conclude that it means no collections are taken up!

All this illustrates how quickly the sufferings and struggles of former generations are forgotten by the religious and irreligious alike, and how the church/chapel divide which fashioned the social structure of English and Welsh community life is almost a thing of the past in this modern ecumenical age. Such ignorance is dangerous, since liberties secured through pain and sacrifice could once again be withdrawn, perhaps in more subtle ways. A previous U.K. Home Secretary, David Blunkett, no doubt with the very best of motives, in an attempt to defuse situations inflamed by those intent on stirring up religious hatred, has labelled what he calls 'far right evangelical Christians' as a potential danger. The post-modern mind denies the very existence of truth, and in our multi-faith society, when non-Christian religions are being indulged for the sake of social harmony, Christians are beginning to discover that Christian distinctives are being regarded as politically incorrect and former liberties are being withdrawn. A Nonconformist minister friend of mine has recently had his ability to speak to the children of a local school withdrawn because he mentioned 'heaven' and stated that we needed Jesus to bring us there!

Magistrates and the imposition of religion

Dissent represented a refusal to conform to a system of church life and worship imposed by law. The freedom for which Dissenters strove was well summarized by Lord John Russell in his House of Commons speech in 1828 proposing the repeal of the Test and Corporation Acts. 'The great principle', he said, motivating pressure for repeal was:

> that every man ought to be allowed to form his religious opinions by the impressions on his own mind, and that, when so formed, he should be at liberty to worship God according to the dictates of his conscience, without being subjected to any penalty or disqualification whatever; that every restraint or restriction imposed on any man on account of his religious creed is in the nature of persecution, and is at once an offence to God, and an injury to man.[2]

This statement requires some qualification. According to Russell, the Dissenters wanted all men to have the freedom to form their own religious views and be permitted to worship according to their consciences. But not all Dissenters were as tolerant as that. In fact, historically, no general agreement had existed among Nonconformists as to what they believed regarding the duties and obligations of civil magistrates and rulers with respect to the practice of religion. One might have expected them to take the view that it is no part of a civil ruler's task to impose any particular religion. But this was certainly not the view of the sixteenth-century Separatists who taught that rulers and magistrates had a duty to encourage the Christian faith as expressed in its central doctrines, to suppress idolatry and to punish wicked behaviour.

The *Westminster Confession of Faith,* agreed upon by the Westminster Assembly of Divines and later ratified by the General Assembly of the Church of Scotland in 1647, went much further, reflecting the influence of the Scottish representatives. In 'Of the Civil Magistrate', it states:

> he hath authority, and it is his duty, to take order ... that the truth of God be kept pure and entire, that all blasphemies and heresies be suppressed, all corruptions and abuses in worship and discipline prevented or reformed, and all the ordinances of God duly settled, administered, and observed. For better effecting whereof, he hath power to call synods, to be present at them, and to provide that whatsoever is transacted in them be according to the mind of God (*Westminster Confession,* xxiii. 3).

Those subscribing to such a view could hardly complain should the magistrate hold a different view from them as to what constituted a blasphemy or a heresy, and inflict persecution upon them.

The Separatists excluded any involvement of the magistrate in church affairs, and so did the Baptists and Independents. But the Independents in their Savoy Declaration of 1658 followed the Separatists in affirming that the magistrate had a duty to protect those professing the gospel and to prevent blasphemy and error that would destroy the souls of the people. They wisely added the rider that the magistrate has no warrant to intervene in matters of 'differences about the Doctrines of the Gospel, or the ways of the worship of God.'

The Particular Baptists in their 1677 *Confession of Faith*, published in 1689, excluded from the duties of the magistrate any responsibility for the maintenance of true religion, confining his God-given responsibility to the 'defence and encouragement of them that do good, and for the punishment of evil doers' (*Baptist Confession of Faith*, 1689, ch. 24.1). In this they followed the lead given by the General Baptists, and in particular by John Smyth in 1612, the first Englishman to be convinced of the need for religious freedom for all Christians. Smyth argued for religious toleration and against the involvement of the magistrates in religious affairs. Thomas Helwys went even further and pleaded for the toleration of *all* men: 'Let them be heretikes, Turcks, Jewes or whatsoever', since, he argued, 'man's religion … is betwixt God and themselves.'[3]

The concept of freedom

In considering the freedom of the Free Churchman, two issues require some clarification. The first is the *concept of freedom*. In modern thinking the idea of freedom has undergone such a change as to require some qualification. Historically, Nonconformists have not envisaged freedom in an autonomous or individualistic way.

The freedom sought by Nonconformists has been a responsible liberty to live and worship in submission to the truth of God's Word, free from any impositions or constraints imposed by the state. He has sought a freedom to be subject to God's Word and to Jesus Christ in the practice of his religious faith. He would not have quarrelled with Harry Blamires' definition that 'Freedom, for the Christian, consists of choosing obedience.'[4]

Nonconformist demands for liberty of worship gave rise from time to time to suspicions of an underlying rebelliousness against the state. They were divided in their allegiances during the Civil War: most supported the Parliamentary cause, but others sided with the king. In those troubled times, whether or not the state was finally vested in Parliament or in the feckless king was a matter of sharp debate. In the 1680s, the Nonconformists were courted by William of Orange, and most were glad to be rid of James II. However, in more settled times Nonconformists have been sensitive to the biblical exhortation to be subject to earthly rulers in those areas of life where God has delegated authority to human governments. Despite this, they have often been suspected of subversive intentions against the state. To call into question the character of the Established Church was frequently interpreted as being an enemy of the realm.

Consequently Nonconformists suffered severe persecution in the 1670s and 1680s, and considerable misrepresentation in 1745, and later, following the French Revolution in 1789. Some elements of the Old Dissent were quite radical and in sympathy with what took place in France, and others with millennial expectations welcomed the developments.[5] Even the New Dissent of the eighteenth-century Evangelical Revival was not beyond suspicion. The use of such phrases as 'The rights of freeborn Englishmen' by Alexander Kilham in the 1790s laid the founder of the Methodist New Connexion open to suspicion and not surprisingly, given the jittery nature of the times, he was called a Painite — after Tom Paine, whose book *The Rights of Man* had caused great alarm. But John Wesley observed, 'We are not republicans, and never intend to be.'[6] This sentiment expressed the conviction of Methodists as a whole and Nonconformists in general. The Wesleyan Methodists regularly reaffirmed their loyalty to king and country at their annual conferences to avoid being suspected of radicalism.

Before 1662 and the Great Ejection of two thousand ministers from the Church of England, visible Dissent was neither extensive nor always clearly defined. The number of Baptist and Independent churches before the outbreak of the Civil War in 1642 was quite small. Those of Congregational conviction were, like the Presbyterians, often found within the parish churches, as were also a few Baptists. The upheaval of the Civil War appeared to be accompanied by a considerable spiritual awakening. But not until after the Great Ejection of 1662 did the distinctive denominational groupings assume a more influential character. We agree with Michael Watts who said:

> sooner or later the Puritan had to choose between con-
> formity and Dissent, and in so far as thousands chose
> the latter course the gain to Dissent was immense ...
> And although the immediate effect of the Restoration
> religious settlement was to bring persecution and suf-
> fering to those outside the Established Church, it can,
> in retrospect, be seen as a step towards the eventual
> and permanent liberation of Dissent.[7]

But how did Dissent cope with persecution and repression by the state? Better than the Scottish Covenanters, who often resorted to arms in striving for religious liberty, contrary to the exhortations of Romans 13:1-5. The Fifth Monarchy rising under Thomas Venner in January 1661 brought increased suffering on the Quakers and Baptists, but subsequently the Dissenters soon learned to heed the wisdom of John Penry, that brilliant star of the sixteenth-century Separatist Movement, who taught that believers should bear persecution, and 'in no wise to withstand the power thereof, either by open force or secret practices.'[8] The Quakers suffered more than most in refusing to compromise on what they felt God required of them. They were at times disruptive on account of their biblical literalism, but Whitefield made a touching comment on their general behaviour: 'The Quakers, though wrong in their principles, yet I think have left us an example of patient suffering, and did more by their bold unanimous and persevering testimonies, than if they had taken up all the arms in the kingdom.'[9]

These were days when the hopes of many Nonconformists for religious liberty were cruelly dashed. With the passing of the Act of Uniformity in 1662 they found themselves thrust into an era of severe persecution. The aspiration for a national church modelled on Presbyterian lines had come to nothing. For others, such as the Fifth Monarchists and groups with similar millennial expectations, their hopes for a heaven on earth had not materialized. Instead, the Free Churchman was beginning to discover the nature of true spiritual freedom in the midst of the severity of his sufferings. No longer did his freedom depend on the right political climate, or upon the whim of the self-indulgent king, and neither was he dependent on the freedom conceded by the tolerance of other men. What he found under the 'Great Persecution' of 1662-1688 was that the freedom of the Free Churchman is found most fully in humble and believing submission to the will and providence of God. This was true even though he was in prison, deprived of all his social liberties, and his family was on the verge of destitution.

This new perspective comes into view in the writings of Nonconformists of those days — such men as Bunyan, Milton, Goodwin, Howe, Manton and Theophilus Gale. Suffering is now seen as the badge of the saint. Baxter expressed it as follows: 'Sufferings must be the Churches most ordinary Lot, and Christians indeed must be self-denying Cross-bearers.' No longer were they, he said, to 'flatter themselves with the Hopes of a Golden Age.'[10] Howe argues that the great work of persecution is to teach self-denial, and its great reward is the gift of spiritual freedom. George Hughes, ejected from the living of St Andrews, Plymouth, wrote, 'Free communion with God in prison is worth a thousand liberties gained with loss of liberty of spirit. The Lord keep us his free men.'[11]

Here then is Nonconformity come of age, the Free Churchman discovering his true freedom. To serve God according to the promptings of one's own conscience, unfettered by ecclesiastical or state impositions in matters of service and worship to God — regardless of the outward cost involved — constituted the essential liberty of the Free Churchman.

As a whole, following 1662, the Dissenters were not only law-abiding citizens, but they also made admirable contributions to the general good of society, despite having to bear considerable injustice. They did not belong to the Church of England, and yet were obliged to pay the Church tithe, despite being frequently denied the benefits to which it legally entitled them.

Nonconformist 'rights' and disabilities

A further issue requiring some clarification is how non-conformists regarded their '*rights*'. They insisted on certain rights which they felt belonged to them by the laws of the land, and when deprived of what they believed were their entitlements as citizens — religiously, socially, educationally and politically — they strove to obtain them. They claimed the liberty to worship God according to their conscience and understanding of God's Word. If they were impeded in what they believed to be their duty before God, then like the apostles of old, they resolved to obey God rather than man.

The concern of the Nonconformist throughout his history has not been for 'human rights' as popularly conceived today. He was concerned with duties rather than rights, and sought the necessary freedom to fulfil those duties before God. But people with strong convictions are inclined to develop tender consciences and to squabble over minor matters, and the Dissenters in those days were given to division over secondary issues as are their evangelical descendants today. Take the question of musical instruments used in worship. Division was as sharp then as it is now, as the following quotation from a certain James Owen in 1700 illustrates. He describes organs and instrumental music in public worship as fit only for 'superstitious Fops, and empty Noddies, a distracting Theatrical Pomp, and Noisie Ostentation.' It is, he continues, 'a sad lame Devotion, that stands in need of a few tweedling Organ-pipes to make it more brisk and lively.'[12] So here we have the modern ultra-traditionalist, wedded to organs, cast in the role of an eighteenth-century Graham Kendrick! Thankfully, when their greater interests were threatened, the Dissenters were able to present a much more united front.

In this connection something must be said about the function and contribution of the Protestant Dissenting Deputies. All Free Church ministers are well-advised to read Bernard Lord Manning's definitive work, *Protestant Dissenting Deputies,* published in 1952, ten years after his death. The Deputies were originally a lay offshoot of what was called the General Body of Ministers which represented three denominations: Presbyterians, Independents (or Congregationalists) and Baptists (both General and Particular). This body of Dissenting ministers had the right of access to the throne with the ability to present addresses to the monarch. They had been accustomed from the time of the Glorious Revolution of 1688 to appear in court to pay their respects. The Protestant Dissenting Deputies, however, was a lay association formed in 1732 to seek the repeal of the Test and Corporation Acts and to protect the civil rights of Dissenters. It still exists today. Dissenting churches in and around the cities of London and Westminster were able to appoint deputies to represent them on this body. Most of the deputies were responsible and influential men able to secure support and representation from members of Parliament and the legal profession of those willing to speak and act on their behalf.

Despite recognition given to Dissenters and their legal right to worship God according to their convictions, in actual practice the Dissenters suffered severe social and educational disabilities, and frequent oppression and persecution. The squire and local vicar in villages and small towns and the landowners of what was largely a rural nation in the eighteenth century exercised a stranglehold upon the community. Where they combined in hostility to Dissent they had considerable intimidatory power at the expense of the Dissenters. Injustices were common. There were cases of deceased Dissenters remaining unburied for months because the local vicar refused permission for them to be interred in the church graveyard with a Nonconformist service which was their legal right. David Lloyd-George shot to national prominence in 1888 when as a young solicitor in Criccieth he was consulted by grieving relatives seeking to bury a loved one in Llanfrothen. Entrance to the church burial ground had been refused by the local rector who had padlocked the gates. What were they to do? 'Tear the gates down!' was the unusual incautious legal advice they received — advice that was later vindicated in the High Court in London.

As late as 1838 two Dissenting Welshmen were sent to prison for not attending the services of the Established Church, and a similar event happened in Kent. Not until the Parliament Bill of 1836[13], declaring that marriage should be regarded as a civil rather than a religious contract, could a Dissenter be legally married in England, except in a parish church by a clergyman of the Church of England. In the years preceding 1836, there were Dissenting couples throughout the country who were not legally married because many local clergymen refused to marry Dissenters. Such couples were often charged with fornication.[14] We can be thankful that their commitment to one another meant that in the sight of God they were nevertheless husband and wife. Even as late as the 1850s and 1860s many Anglican clergy refused to accept the validity of Nonconformist marriages. The law was one thing, but the implementation of it was quite another. In days when communications were extremely slow, Dissenters suffered much abuse and injustice. To such cases the Protestant Dissenting Deputies applied themselves to secure justice for oppressed Dissenters.

Before 1828, no civil or military office or any position of trust under the crown could be held unless the officeholder received the sacrament of the Lord's Supper according to the rites of the Church of England, and despite the repeal of the Test and Corporation Acts in that same year, Dissenters remained under considerable restraint. Admission to Oxford and Cambridge Universities was not possible for Dissenters until the mid 1850s, and even then it was not until 1871 that the religious declaration of loyalty to the Church of England was abolished as a condition of obtaining a degree in Oxford, Cambridge or Durham. So three cheers for London University, founded by royal charter in 1836 which was, as the then Chancellor of the Exchequer, Mr Spring Rice, expressed it, 'freed from those exclusions and religious distinctions which abridge the usefulness of Oxford and of Cambridge.'

Not until the twentieth century did our Nonconformist forebears enjoy the legal rights and freedom we tend to take for granted. One irony of the situation was that Jews, Quakers and frequently Roman Catholics had more privileges and indulgences granted to them by law in the eighteenth and nineteenth centuries than the Dissenters. So next time you see the notice 'Free Church' be thankful to God for the religious liberty and freedom of worship you now enjoy.

Nonconformist views regarding the relationship between Church and State

We have taken note of a variety of views held by Nonconformists as to the responsibility of the civil magistrates with regards to the church. We need to open this out a little, and consider in general Nonconformist views regarding the relationship between church and state.

The weakness of some Nonconformist bodies, such as the Scottish Presbyterians, has been their insistence upon the duty of the state to uphold true religion. But how they expected the spiritually unenlightened to discern and distinguish truth from error has never satisfactorily been explained.

The impracticability of this position is increasingly evident today in the development of a multi-cultural and multi-faith society within a so-called 'Christian' country. The dependence of some on Isaiah 49:22-23 which speaks of kings being Israel's 'foster fathers' and queens their 'foster mothers' has always looked implausible when applied to the church in the context of the New Testament and set within the religious hodgepodge of Roman society.

The biblical justification for the Nonconformist position (whether Independent or Presbyterian) that the church should be a self-governing body within society, free from the interference of the state, and yet respecting the laws and administration of the state, arises from the fact that the Christian is seen to be a citizen of two distinct kingdoms. He is a citizen of the state to which he belongs by natural birth, but he is also a citizen of the kingdom of God by spiritual rebirth, as expressed in the life of the gathered church. These two kingdoms are quite distinct: the one being a national state within this fallen world, ordered and preserved by the common grace of God, and the other being a spiritual kingdom of God brought into existence by special grace. Of this kingdom Jesus declared, 'My kingdom is not of this world' (John 18:36). The principles by which the spiritual kingdom is brought into being and governed are not the same as those by which the kingdoms of this world are governed. They are of a higher and spiritual order, which the children of this world can neither understand nor implement.

But the believer's transition from the kingdom of darkness to the kingdom of light does not release him from his obligations and duties as a citizen of his earthly kingdom. He is commanded to 'be subject to governing authorities' because such powers are 'not a terror to good conduct, but to bad' (Rom. 13:1-3). The reason for this should be obvious: the maintenance of law and order and the suppression of anarchy and criminality are always in the self-interest of rulers and governing authorities however wicked or corrupt they might be.

The believer is also commanded to respect and honour earthly rulers. He is told to 'honour the king' (1 Pet. 2:17), to be a law-abiding and dutiful citizen (Rom. 13:7; 1 Pet. 2:13-17), and to pray for all those in authority over him (1 Tim. 2:1-3). Love for all men is to be the prevailing motivation for his obedience to those in authority, and his concern for the well-being of his fellow men (Rom. 13:10). He should guard against the temptation of bad-mouthing politicians and those in authority over him, such as members of the government or the police.

The Christian's subjection to human governments and magistrates and his respect for local and national laws should arise from recognition that such authority has been delegated to men by God. The living God is the One to whom the believer renders ultimate obedience; should the state and its officers trespass from their civil duties into the spiritual realm, where it has no legitimate authority, then the Christian is to obey the higher power. This was the consistent position of the Nonconformists. Like Daniel and his friends, Shadrach, Meshach and Abednego, they were not prepared to deny their faith, nor would they conform to a state church which they believed was biblically in error. Rather than submit, they were prepared to suffer persecution and imprisonment. And if ordered by the secular authority to remain silent as to the truth of the gospel, as were John Bunyan and Isaac Watts senior, then with Peter and John they chose 'to obey God rather than men' (Acts 5:29; 4:19, 20). If the voice of established religion sought to suppress their testimony, then like the apostles who were commanded by God to 'Go and stand in the temple and speak to the people all the words of this life' (Acts 5:20), they too bore their testimony to the truth. Some, such as Henry Barrowe, John Greenwood and John Penry in 1593, suffered death in consequence. If, contrary to the law, those appointed to uphold the law ceased to do so, then the Nonconformists in common with the Apostle Paul (Acts 16:35-39; 22:25) did not hesitate to appeal to the law. Much of the work of the Protestant Dissenting Deputies was of this nature, insisting that existing laws be respected and implemented.

The Nonconformist conviction that the Christian is a citizen of two distinct kingdoms was based on the teaching of the New Testament. They did not confuse the situation of Israel in the Old Testament, where the civil and spiritual kingdoms were formally equated with that which should prevail under the new covenant. They recognized a measure of continuity between the Old and New Testaments, but also stood with Paul in affirming the discontinuity. Unlike Israel of old, the church is not to be equated with society in general — as was the Church of England until fairly recent times. The unique position of Israel as the chosen people of God, being a political as well as a spiritual entity, no longer applies under the new covenant. From Pentecost onwards the distinctive feature of the new Israel, as distinct from the old, is that the church is a regenerate society. What should distinguish the new covenant people from old covenant Israel is that, as predicted by Jeremiah, 'They shall all know me, from the least of them to the greatest of them, says the Lord' (Jer. 31:34). This concept of the church as a gathered community of true believers, existing within society and yet distinct from it, has governed the thinking of Dissenters through the centuries. Michael Watts comments: 'If Dissent involved separation from the Church of England, far more did it imply separation from the world.'[15]

The freedom of the Free Churchman is a freedom to gather in worship and fellowship with those of like mind and spiritual life, free from any imposition by external authority or national church, and to do this in obedience to the Word of God with a clear conscience.

When the Puritans, suffering within the Established Church of England in the early seventeenth century due to its half-reformed character, emigrated to the New World they were able to establish churches of a biblical character. But they eventually got into difficulties because the churches sought to impose upon the whole community principles and a pattern of behaviour characteristic of the regenerate man. They used their newfound liberty to deny others the very freedom that they had sought for themselves. Learning lessons from their bitter experience, the United States introduced into its Constitution, implemented in 1789, an article securing the independence of the state from any particular religious commitment and guaranteeing its citizens the free exercise of religion.

Modern application and lessons

A number of the issues upon which I have touched deserve papers in their own right. I have only been able to produce a survey under the general title 'The Freedom of the Free Churchman'. Many of the struggles and battles fought by our Nonconformist forefathers are no longer burning issues: liberty of worship, political and social entitlements, and the vexed issue of the involvement of the Established Church in education. But these struggles ought not to be forgotten, because ignorance of our past will be sure to catch us unawares.

One present danger is for Christians to equate spiritual freedom with the autonomy of the individual — a socially destructive concept prevalent in our modern society which has to some extent influenced our churches. It has no support in Scripture. The spiritual freedom of the Christian is a freedom from the tyranny of sin and Satan, secured for him by the intervention and power of Jesus Christ. Christian churches and their members do not have a liberty to 'do their own thing'. Deliverance from the oppression of Satan places believers under the Lordship of Jesus Christ and subject to the authority of God as expressed in his Holy Word. We are free to obey.

The word 'Nonconformist' suggests a person who refuses to yield to external pressure to fall into line. Our Nonconformist forefathers were intent on obeying their consciences as informed by the Word of God — to worship according to the mind of God and not to yield to the dictates of the throne or the government of the Established Church seeking to impose unbiblical requirements. They were *Non*-conformists because they were men of biblical principle. No longer are we under the pressures they suffered, and thanks to the resolute stand they took, we enjoy religious liberty at present. But has our liberty and freedom made us stronger? Or has the removal of past constraints and persecution put us off our guard: ecumenically, educationally and socially?

I have a feeling that the modern liking for a tolerance which regards all religions as equally valid and makes no moral demands upon us is a growing threat to our religious liberties. This modern mood, associated with an increasing liking for a comfortable religion within our churches, nurtures a strong dislike of those principles which motivated our Nonconformist forefathers. Within Nonconformist evangelicalism today a truce appears to have been declared over such issues as the nature of a true church and the importance of distinguishing between truth and error. Opposition to false ecumenicity has become muted of late, increasing emphasis is being placed on horizontal and social concerns, and we are no longer being urged to separate from those who deny the faith. This blurring of issues is characteristic of our day, but the time will come when those who take a resolute stand upon biblical principles will again be persecuted for their convictions.

The Nonconformist struggle for freedom and the exercise of legitimate rights was strengthened towards the end of the eighteenth century and in the first fifty years of the nineteenth century by a series of revivals of religion. These affected the Methodists, Baptists and Congregationalists and greatly increased their numbers and influence within the nation. In this period the number of Nonconformist chapels multiplied tenfold. The successful outcome of Wilberforce's anti-slavery campaign in 1833, after forty-five years of persistent, and largely unsuccessful, campaigning, was not so much due to Wilberforce and his friends as to the changed mood within the nation, resulting from the widespread growth of Nonconformity. This change was noted by Lord John Russell in his parliamentary speech of 1828 proposing the repeal of the Test and Corporation Acts.[16] Within Nonconformist churches a place had been given to the common man, which was denied him in society as a whole. The Nonconformist struggle for religious equality and liberty created a climate in which social, educational and political rights were progressively obtained. True democratic ideals were given increasing recognition, and eventually this led to acceptance of workers' unions, enlarged political franchise and equality of educational opportunity. Our democratic form of government has its roots within Nonconformity and developed alongside the Nonconformist struggle for liberty and recognition; it can be argued that it is a by-product of it. The autocratic power of the nobility and squirearchy of the Established Church had been challenged and weakened. Pressure to conform had been reluctantly relaxed, but only reluctantly since privilege is not readily surrendered.

One of the present dangers for our nation is that the weakening of the Nonconformist presence, conscience, and influence, and the almost complete institutional collapse of Nonconformity, has left an ideological vacuum within our society in which new forms of totalitarianism might well emerge to rob us of the immense gains secured by our Nonconformist forefathers. There appears to be a drift taking place within our Free Evangelical churches towards a rapprochement with the Established Church. The Anglicans have not been slow to take advantage of this. But we need to be aware of the fact that the Established Church comprehends within its boundaries people of all religious and moral hues, and with the breakdown of evangelicalism which refuses to collaborate with those that deny the faith, there arises the threat of an ecumenical totalitarianism which cannot endure any who will not conform. One must never forget that a national church has always been a persecuting church.

I have always had a lingering admiration for George Fox. N. H. Keeble describes him as 'the greatest religious genius of his age'. There is a measure of truth there. He was an awkward individual and a somewhat disruptive influence. He held views on 'the inner light' which took him beyond Scripture; but what I admire in Fox is his immediacy, his strength of resolution and his courageous Nonconformity. We would benefit from a little of that spirit today, plunged into a biblical mould.

Chapter 2

The Roots of Nonconformity

Robert Oliver

The late Professor G. M. Trevelyan considered the year 1559 to be the year of the birth of modern England and Scotland. In England it was the year of the Elizabethan Church Settlement, while in Scotland that of John Knox's sudden return to his country and the subsequent establishment of a Presbyterian church there. The Elizabethan age has been described as one of the most creative periods in English history. In those years, religious Dissent, later to be known as Nonconformity, became a serious player in English religious life.

The early Nonconformists

The roots of Nonconformity strike deeply into the soil of the English Reformation, and indeed of earlier movements as well. If the Elizabethan Settlement of 1559 gave the Church of England its definitive form, there was even at that date an articulate body of Protestant Christians who were convinced that there was still much to do if the church were to reflect the pattern of the New Testament. Probably most of these men hoped that they could advance the cause of Reformation from within the bounds of the Established Church. The brief reign of Edward VI from 1547 to 1553 had been a time of steady advance for the Protestants; why should the same not be true for the reign of Edward's half-sister Elizabeth? The persecution under Mary I which had intervened between those two reigns had wiped out much of the leadership of Edward's church. If

Elizabeth were to establish a Protestant church in England, she had to draw upon younger men to supply its ministry. Many of this new generation, exiles in Mary's reign, had experienced a more vigorous Protestantism in Germany and Switzerland. They returned to England with high hopes of a bright future for the English church. To begin, there were ceremonies and practices which had associations with the unreformed Church of Rome. It would surely be a simple matter to remove these and to bring English practice into line with that of the reformed churches of the continent. The practices to which they objected included wearing the surplice, making the sign of the cross in baptism and kneeling to receive the Lord's Supper. The list can be extended. Some of these objections were to what were seen as the relics of 'popery', but there was a growing resentment to the imposition of man-made ceremonies in public worship. Soon there were added to these demands pressure for a more efficient form of church discipline which would safeguard the purity of the sacraments at the local level.

Queen Elizabeth had no desire for further reform; through her ministers and bishops she blocked attempts to bring about changes. Those who ignored the settlement of 1559 and the way it was enforced by successive archbishops faced heavy penalties. Although the hand of authority became increasingly heavy as the years passed, many who refused to conform were able to continue their ministries in the Church of England. They were the first to be described as Nonconformists. John Owen's father, Henry, was such a minister in the Established Church of England. Of him his son John could write in 1657, 'my father … was a Nonconformist all his days'.[1]

It is important to note that before 1660 the men who were described as Nonconformists were ministers who were resolved to continue their ministry within the Church of England. Some eleven years before Owen wrote these words, there appeared a tract by John Geere entitled, *The Character of an Old English Puritane or Nonconformist* (1646). Geere clearly equated Nonconformity with Puritanism, writing: 'just laws and commands he willingly obeyed … but such as were unjust he refused to observe, choosing to obey God rather than man: yet his refusal was modest and with submission to penalties, unless he could procure indulgence from authority'.[2]

Although Geere's Nonconformist believed in church discipline, he did not think that the way forward was to separate from the Established Church. He went on, 'the corruptions that were in the churches he thought it his duty to bewail, with endeavours of amendment, yet he would not separate'.

Geere's words indicate that there were those who did separate from the Church of England and to them we must turn.

The Separatists

The Lollard tradition

There is a long-standing Separatist tradition deeply rooted in England reaching back before the Reformation. It can certainly be traced back to the followers of John Wyclif known as Lollards. Wyclif, who died in 1384, had been a lecturer and outstanding scholar in the University of Oxford. His collision with the authorities began with an attack on the abuses of clerical power and privilege, but moved on to an attack on the doctrines of transubstantiation and indulgences. He insisted on the Christian's direct access to God through Christ. For his alleged heresies he was deprived of his teaching role at Oxford, although he continued to minister and direct his followers from his parish in the little Leicestershire town of Lutterworth. It was Wyclif's ministry that inspired the production of the Bible in the English language. Translated from the Latin Vulgate by his close associates it appeared in manuscript copies from the 1380s.

Wyclif himself remained a priest within the Roman Church throughout his life, but it was not long before his followers were meeting in unofficial and illegal groups. In some cases these may have been informal meetings supplementing regular attendance at the parish churches, but certainly in others Lollards withdrew from services of the recognized church. In spite of the fact that, from 1401, Lollardy was a capital offence which was punishable by death by burning, the Lollards were never wiped out by the authorities.

The early Tudor period, 1485-1558

In spite of persecution, Lollardy continued. Some were being brought before the courts as late as the reign of Henry VIII (1509-1547). Towards the end of his reign, it becomes more difficult to distinguish the Lollards from the Protestant groups springing up under the impact of the Reformation. Henry VIII broke English allegiance to Rome for political reasons, but in doctrine remained a Romanist until his dying day. Throughout the latter years of his reign, those who asserted their allegiance to the papacy could be executed for treason, while those who believed Protestant doctrines were in danger of being burned for heresy.

In the short reign of Edward VI (1547-1553), the Church of England assumed a Protestant form: services were in the vernacular, the mass was abolished, worship was simplified and preaching became evangelical. It did however retain the medieval structure of government by bishops, sustained by ancient laws, courts and functionaries. English citizens were required to attend the services of the Reformed Church of England.

However in spite of the protests of his bishops, Edward VI granted a charter to foreign Protestants in London under the leadership of the Polish reformer John à Lasco in July 1550. The charter recognized a church with its own powers of government and freedom to elect its own officers. Londoners were provided with a model of a working independent church in action. Another church of French exiles was set up at Glastonbury in Somerset under the leadership of Valerand Poullain à Fleming, who had served in Strasbourg. These two congregations appear to have been the first two independent churches set up with royal approval. The early death of Edward VI in the summer of 1553 terminated these two experiments.

The reign of Mary I (1553-1558) was one of Roman Catholic reaction against the reforms of her brother Edward VI. Under Mary a considerable number of wealthier Protestants and leaders were able to take refuge on the continent. There they came into contact with more thoroughly reformed churches than they had known in England. We have already noted their expectation of immediate advance after their return. Instead, hopes were dashed and a protracted struggle ensued.

Radical reformers

There were other Protestants who had not been able to escape during Mary's reign. From this group the martyrs were drawn. Some of these met secretly for worship. In London such a group became known as the 'privy' or secret church. One of their pastors, John Rough, and a deacon, Cuthbert Simson, were arrested at the Saracen's Head in Islington where the congregation had come together. Just before his execution Rough wrote to the group whom he described as 'the Congregation'. In his letter he reminded them, 'Ye are not without the great Pastor of your soul, who so loveth you, that if men were not to be sought out (as God be praised there is no want of men), he would cause stones to minister unto you'.[3]

After Rough's arrest, the congregation received as minister Thomas Bentham, who returned from exile in Germany to minister to them. In July 1558 he wrote to a friend in Switzerland:

> While I was in Germany, at liberty of body ... I was yet many times in great grief of mind, and terrible torments of hell; and now here being every moment of an hour in danger of taking, and fear of bodily death, I am in mind, the Lord be praised, most quiet and joyful seeing the fervent zeal of many, and such increase of our congregation even in the midst of this cruel and violent persecution.[4]

Later generations of Separatists looked back to these secret congregations as providing precedents for their own Independency. They pointed out that John Rough had an honoured place in Foxe's *Acts and Monuments*. It is only fair to note that John Rough had been ordained in the Church of England during the reign of Edward VI. There is also evidence that, in the reign of Mary, he conducted secret worship at Colchester in Essex using

the second Prayer Book of Edward VI. What the practice of the
London congregation was in this respect we do not know.

As the tardiness of reformation bred frustration, in the 1560s
some bolder spirits recalled the precedent of secret worship. In
1567, an illegal meeting of about 100 people was discovered at
Plumbers' Hall in London. They had hired the building under
pretext of a wedding. The leaders were brought before Bishop
Grindal then of London. They insisted that they were not opposed to the Church of England as such, but they found some
of its practices intolerable. They told the bishop, 'we remembered that there was a congregation of us in this city in Queen
Mary's days'.[5] Grindal, who himself sympathized with many of
their aspirations, pointed out that the Marian martyrs had worn
the surplice to which they objected. Their spokesman William
Nixon replied, 'We condemn them not: we would go forward
to perfection; for we have had the Gospel a long time amongst
us; and the best of them that did maintain it, did recant for it
at their death, as did Ridley ... and Doctor Taylor'.[6] For their
Dissent, a number of those arrested spent almost two years in
the Bridewell.

In his analysis of the records of their trials, Patrick Collinson
points out that the accused kept referring to: 'our preachers!
Your law, your courts and your apparel!' He makes the point
that these people were already virtual sectarians. 'Their attach-
ment was to their preachers ... not to the parish church.' The
only qualification was that they had not seceded irrevocably.
They would go to church if they could 'hear sound preachers
who were not obliged to wear "idolatrous gear"'. They had tak-
en no steps to elect their own officers or set up their own church
organization. One of the Separatists told John Knox that these
illegal meetings 'brought many a hundred to know one another
that never knew before'.[7]

The Separatists

The name Robert Browne will always be associated with organized Separatism, although he was a Separatist for only a short
time in a long career. Robert Browne was born near Stamford

in Lincolnshire, a distant relative of Elizabeth's great minister William Cecil. He went up to Cambridge at a time when Thomas Cartwright, Lady Margaret Professor of Divinity, was challenging the organization of the Church of England in a series of lectures on the Acts of the Apostles. Cartwright was eventually forced out of the university, but his lecturing and writings entitle him to be considered one of the founders of English Presbyterianism. Browne completed his studies at Cambridge and went on to ordination in the Church of England. At some point he reached the conclusion that the structure of the Church of England was at fault. From an Anglican pulpit in Cambridge he declared that bishops were 'ravenous and wicked persons who sought rather their own advantage or glory, or mischievous purpose, than the benefit of the church'. At this point Robert Harrison, an old undergraduate friend who was a hospital chaplain in Norwich, met up with him and suggested that it might be better for him to live in Norwich than Cambridge. Browne accepted and went to live in Norwich as Harrison's paying guest.

Harrison was already in touch with a number of radicals who were uneasy with the spiritual provision of the parish churches. Under the leadership of Robert Browne and Robert Harrison they concluded that *the rule of the bishops and the whole organization of the Church of England with its parish system was wrong.* Inevitably they too fell foul of the authorities who were alarmed to find Browne preaching to a conventicle of about 100 in Bury St Edmunds. From these meetings a group led by Browne and Harrison emigrated to the Netherlands in 1581. Browne continued to study ecclesiology; he published his views in 1582 under the title, *A Treatise of Reformation Without Tarrying for Any.* He concluded that the proper basis of a church was a *covenant* between its members. He wrote, 'the Lord's people is of the willing sort'. The church members would elect their officers. These received their authority from God, but were called by the members. The civil authorities could not impose ministers or plant churches. Unlike the Continental Anabaptists, he did not argue for a complete separation of church and state. Browne believed that the state should care for the true church and so it had the authority to put down false religion. He argued that the overthrow of the Roman Catholic Church in England by royal authority was a justified use of the power of the state.

Browne's attitude towards the Church of England was that it was utterly corrupt and that true believers should have nothing to do with it. Harrison on the other hand believed that there were genuine believers and ministers within its ranks and that fellowship with these was possible. Harrison also looked to the state to further the work of reformation. Tensions developed, with Harrison accusing Browne of 'antichristian pride and bitterness'. Browne left for Scotland, but discovered Presbyterianism to be as uncongenial as Episcopacy. He returned to England, where he eventually conformed to the Church of England and for many years served as a parish minister, albeit with a somewhat stormy career. Ironically Separatism was long described as Brownism, whereas Robert Browne himself was treated by his former colleagues as an apostate. Browne is however important because he published a systematic exposition of his teaching, which continued to guide men after he himself had ceased to be a Separatist. Harrison lived only a few years after the departure of Browne, but Separatism was to receive a fresh impetus in England.

There were still Separatist movements in London. From the mid-1580s, Archbishop John Whitgift set about rooting out Puritanism from the Church of England with a fresh zeal. As a result, a number of men were deprived. These included John Greenwood, a Norfolk clergyman who made his way to London where he joined the Separatists. In 1586 he was arrested at a meeting. While in prison he was visited by Henry Barrow, an erstwhile lawyer who at one time had some associations with the court of the queen. Having been converted from his worldly lifestyle, he sought out Greenwood, but he did not escape the hawk-like eyes of the Archbishop, who had him arrested while making a prison visit to his friend. The two friends kept up a steady stream of propaganda from prison, even though the authorities tried to keep pen and ink from them. They argued that the worship of the Church of England was disorderly, its membership profane, its ministry false and that it was ruled by an antichristian and ungodly government. Barrow did however concede that the government had a duty to suppress false religion and promote the true. Their books were published in the Netherlands. In March 1593, they were convicted of publishing seditious books. They were hanged at Tyburn in April.

Meanwhile the English ambassador to the Netherlands was charged with the responsibility of hunting down the books of Barrow and Greenwood and destroying them. He enlisted the aid of Francis Johnson, the anti-Separatist chaplain to the expatriate merchants at Middelburg. Overcome by curiosity, Johnson kept two books and read them. He was impressed and returned to London to visit Barrow and Greenwood in prison. As a result, he joined the London Separatist church and was elected pastor in September 1592.

In the meantime, the Separatists gained another distinguished recruit, John Penry. Penry, a Welshman, was a graduate of both Oxford and Cambridge, with a deep burden for the spiritual needs of Wales. Appalled by the indifference of the bishops, he eventually turned to Separatism. Both Johnson and Penry were arrested in 1593. Penry was suspected of having a hand in the publication of the Marprelate Tracts. These were a series of secretly printed anonymous tracts which ridiculed the bishops and their ways. In the words of one historian, Martin Marprelate 'swept away in a tide of unrestrained jocularity all the traditional reverence for the episcopate'.[8] John Penry may have had some involvement in the affair, but any suggestion that he was the author has never been proven. He was however charged with sedition and found guilty; in May 1593 he followed Barrow and Greenwood to the scaffold. At his trial he declared, 'Imprisonment, judgement, yea death itself are not meet weapons to convince men's consciences, grounded on the word of God'.[9] Penry bequeathed a Bible to each of his three small daughters. He ended his will with the words, 'I leave the success of my labours, the calling of my country to the knowledge of Christ's blessed Gospel unto such of my countrymen as the Lord is to raise after me.'[10]

In April 1593 there was passed *An Act for Retaining the Queen's Subjects in Their Due Obedience*. Anyone over the age of sixteen who did not attend church for a month or attended unauthorized religious meetings was liable to imprisonment. If they did not conform within three months, they were to be offered the alternatives of exile or death. Johnson's church chose exile and eventually arrived in Amsterdam where they became known as the 'Antient Church'. In 1597, Johnson was released and eventually able to join them.

As has so often happened in exiled communities, lively debates and controversies developed. One particularly contentious member was *John Smyth* who eventually led a group away from the Antient Church over issues of worship. Some time after his departure Smyth repudiated infant baptism and baptized himself and then his church members. He has been described as the *Se-baptist*. His action was vigorously attacked and he had qualms about self-baptism. He therefore applied to the Waterlanders, a group of Dutch Mennonites, for baptism, which they granted. At the same time he made it clear that he agreed with the Mennonites in their rejection of the Calvinistic doctrines of grace. Thereby he parted company with the main body of English Separatists, who were firm in their belief in the doctrines of grace. The Separatists had published a Confession of Faith in 1596. It was entitled *A True Confession*. Its teaching on salvation is strongly Calvinistic and in its Christology it is orthodox. Smyth and his friend Thomas Helwys must be regarded as the pioneers of the English General Baptists with roots in both Separatism and Anabaptism.

Soon after changing his position on baptism Smyth advanced a plea for toleration stronger than anything the Separatists had so far broached. As late as 1607 he had insisted on the right of magistrates to establish churches and to expect their subjects to join them. In 1612 he wrote,

> The magistrate is not by virtue of his office to meddle with religion, or matters of conscience, to force and compel men to this or that form of religion or doctrine; but to leave Christian religion free, to every man's

conscience, and to handle only civil transgressions, injuries, and the wrongs of men against men.[11]

Smyth died in 1612, but his teachings were brought back to England by Thomas Helwys and his friends, who established a General Baptist Church in Spitalfields in London. He appealed to James I for toleration in terms broader than those of John Smyth. 'Men's religion ... is betwixt God and themselves', and the king cannot judge 'between God and man ... Let them be heretics, Turks, Jews, or whatsoever, it appertains not to the earthly power to punish them'.[12] A widespread fear of 'Anabaptism' which went back to the Munster affair in 1535 perhaps prevented Smyth's and Helwys' views on toleration from receiving proper consideration.

The 'Jacobites'

Henry Jacob (c. 1563-1624)

We need to turn to a movement parallel to Separatism taking place within the ranks of Puritanism. Henry Jacob, a graduate of the University of Oxford, began his career as a minister of the Church of England with Puritan views, and a very real fear of Separatism. During the 1590s, he visited Francis Johnson in prison to try to win him back to his old position. He was, however, influenced more than he had anticipated, although he was not won to Johnson's Separatism. In 1604 he published *Reasons ... for Reforming our Church in England*, in which he made the following four points:

1. Only a congregation of Christians is a New Testament church.
2. Such a church should be gathered by the free consent of believers who covenant to live together as members of a holy society.
3. Since every congregation of faithful people is a proper church, it is not necessary to renounce communion with the Church of England.

4. Every pastor of such a church who cares for his flock in
   a scriptural way is a true pastor.

Jacob insisted that he was not a Separatist. Unlike most
Separatists he did not insist that members of a gathered
church should refuse to listen to preachers in the Church of
England. It has been difficult to classify his position. Champlin
Burrage called him an 'Independent Puritan', Perry Miller a
'Non-Separatist Congregationalist', and Geoffrey Nuttall a
'Semi-Separatist'. Michael Watts argues that all of the above
are wrong. The first two are anachronistic and the third would
have been rejected by Jacob who insisted that he was not a
Separatist. He therefore plumped for *Jacobite* — the contem-
porary term. [13]

Jacob's teaching proved attractive to a number including
William Bradshaw, who became apologist for the movement,
Paul Baynes, Robert Parker and William Ames, its outstanding
theologian.

William Ames (1576-1633) is an interesting figure in the
story. After a brilliant career at Cambridge, where he was converted under the ministry of William Perkins, he was forced out
of the university in 1610 and his degrees were suspended. His
crime was Puritanism. He crossed to the Netherlands where he
was given a post in the University of Leiden. He later played
a significant role in the Synod of Dordt. He became a professor in a new university in Friesland, but here his emphasis on
practical godliness caused him once again to be forced out of
office. He then became pastor of an Independent church in
Rotterdam. His lasting memorial is his *Medulla Theologiae* or
Marrow of Theology published in 1627. As a university tutor
he had attempted to 'call students away from questions and
controversies obscure, confused and not very essential, and introduce it to life and practice so that the students would begin
to think seriously of conscience and its concerns'. [14] He began
his *Medulla* with the words, 'Theology is the doctrine of living
to God'.

William Bradshaw attempted to put the case for the Jacobite
view of the church. He unsuccessfully petitioned James I for

permission to set up such churches which would avow their loyalty to the crown and not threaten the king or the Established Church in the way that Presbyterianism was perceived to do.

The time spent by Jacob, Parker and Ames at Leyden in the Netherlands gave them opportunity for contact with *John Robinson,* pastor of the 'Pilgrim Fathers' church, who modified his extreme Separatism which had rejected contact with the Puritan preachers still in the Church of England.

Jacob returned to England where he established a church in Southwark, which was willing to extend fellowship to members of the Church of England on the one hand and Separatists on the other. Sadly he found himself under fire from both parties. In the 1620s, Jacob left for New England, but his church continued and there was growing support for his position.

The Jacobite position seemed to fit the needs of the English situation

Earlier Puritans who followed Thomas Cartwright had hoped to introduce Presbyterianism. They accepted the concept of a state church, but wanted to introduce a godly discipline. Henry Barrow had objected that they would 'still have the whole land to be the Church and every parish therein to be a particular congregation.' The Presbyterians wanted more power for the congregations, but believed that this would be modified by the power of the eldership and by a hierarchy of assemblies. The investigation of the Marprelate Tracts uncovered an embryonic Presbyterian organization which was suppressed. Puritanism survived where it could be implemented at the parish level. That was possible where congregations had some say in the appointment of ministers and lecturers. Such a system could fit with Jacobite ideas. The Separatists on the other hand accepted the leadership of the officers but insisted that ultimately the authority rested in the congregation. Barrow believed that, in the long run, Presbyterian synods would prove to be as oppressive as the Court of High Commission, which was used by the Church of England bishops against the Puritans.

The development of Jacobite Independency

William Laud, who became archbishop of Canterbury in 1633, implemented a vigorous anti-Puritan campaign. Before he became archbishop he had been a champion of Arminianism and promoter of elaborate ceremonial unknown in the Church of England since the Reformation. His policies forced many Puritans out of their livings in the Church of England. A number of these men fled to the Netherlands, where they organized churches on Jacobite lines. Their leaders included Hugh Peters, Thomas Hooker, William Bridge, Jeremiah Burroughs and Thomas Goodwin. The English government put pressure on the Dutch to compel churches of English expatriates to conform either to the Church of England or to the Dutch Reformed church (Presbyterian). This led to a further exodus to North America. Those who crossed the Atlantic included Thomas Hooker, John Cotton and John Lathrop, who had succeeded Henry Jacob as pastor in Southwark. Cotton's writings were to prove of great importance in the development of Independency in the years after 1640. John Owen was won for Independency by his study of the writings of John Cotton.

Meanwhile, around 1630, a group from the Jacobite church in Southwark adopted stricter Separatist views and questioned the validity of baptism administered in the Church of England. This seems to have developed into a wider review of baptismal theology, leading to them to adopt the practice of believers' baptism only, and that by immersion. This group was granted an amicable separation from the Jacobite church and formed themselves into a Baptist church north of the river in Wapping. Unlike the General Baptist churches already established, they retained the Calvinistic teaching of the Separatists and so may be regarded as the first English Particular or Calvinistic Baptist church. They were led by Samuel Eaton and John Spilsbury. Eaton died in Newgate in 1639, but Spilsbury continued to lead the church until his death in 1668. The Jacobite church continued under the leadership of Henry Jessey, who, along with many of his church members, also adopted Baptist beliefs, but at the same time maintained his Jacobite sympathies.

Impact of the interregnum

The Parliamentary Puritan Revolution, followed by the Parliamentary victory in the Civil Wars, ended the pressure on Puritan ministers within the Church of England. In 1642, Parliament swept away the bishops from the Church of England, but put nothing in their place. Since in the Church of England ordination was the prerogative of the bishops, the future of the ministry was uncertain if no new measures were adopted. Many Anglican Puritans who feared the fragmentation associated with Separatism were drawn towards Presbyterianism, but they lacked any practical experience of its operation. The involvement of the Scots in English politics and the calling of the Westminster Assembly strengthened the resurgence of English Presbyterianism, which of course was prescribed in the documents of the Westminster Assembly. By the end of the Civil War, there was not the political will to implement a Presbyterian structure throughout the country although there were local attempts. Parliament and the government of Oliver Cromwell were more concerned to remove ineffective ministers and replace them by godly men of varying views on church government.

During the Civil War Cromwell rebuked a subordinate for suspending an officer who was alleged to be unorthodox:

> Give me leave to tell you, I cannot be of your judgement; cannot understand it, if a man notorious for wickedness, for oaths, for drinking, hath as great a share in your affection as one that fears an oath, who fears to sin. Aye, but the man is an Anabaptist. Are you sure of that? Admit that he shall be, shall that render him incapable to serve the public? Sir, the State in choosing men to serve it takes no notice of their opinions; if they be willing faithfully to serve it, that satisfies.[15]

In 1653, after Cromwell had effectively become Head of State, in a speech to the leading politicians at Whitehall he said:

We should be pitiful ... that we may have a respect unto
all, and be pitiful and tender towards all though of different judgements ... Love all, be tender to all, cherish
and countenance all, in all things that are good. And
if the poorest Christian, the most mistaken Christian,
shall desire to live peaceably and quietly under you — I
say, if any shall desire to live peaceably and quietly under you — I say, if any shall desire but to lead a life of
godliness and honesty, let him be protected.[16]

The years between 1640 saw a proliferation of sects, orthodox
and unorthodox. Separatists continued to increase and tend-
ed to merge with the Jacobites as Independents. Baptists of
both persuasions and others established churches. In the parish churches, Presbyterians and Independents, as well as a few
Baptists, ministered, as did some crypto-Anglicans. There was a
measure of chaos in the situation, and sadly, a lack of love and
understanding between groups which had much in common.
Evangelical Christians were not prepared for what happened
after the death of Oliver Cromwell in 1658. When the strong
hand of the Lord Protector was removed, there was a breakdown in government; a latent desire for the restoration of the
monarchy broke through in powerful expression. It was an old
and tried form of government and had often worked well in the
past. So it was that, in the early months of 1660, Charles Stuart
was invited to the throne of his father as Charles II. He came
back with the promise of 'a liberty to tender consciences'.

The Restoration

The years 1640 to 1660 left Puritanism divided and facing
the prospect of the restoration of the monarchy with widely
different aspirations. Presbyterians who perhaps thought of
themselves as Nonconformists in the old sense often had no
desire to become Dissenters. They hoped that they might find
a place within the restored Church of England. Independents
generally had no hopes of this, but they did hope that they
might be tolerated outside the Established Church. Both were

disappointed. The laws were framed in such a way that there was much less room for deviation in the state church than there had been before the Civil War. The result was the Great Ejection of 1662 when some two thousand men, many of whom might have served in the church before 1640, were forced out. They joined those whose principles compelled them to reject a state church. The old Nonconformists had become Dissenters. In fact the laws passed after 1660 made them such, although it was a long time before they could recognize this.

John Howe wrote: 'It is not to be thought but among so many parties as come under one common notion of Dissenters from the public rule (and whom that rule did not find *one*, but made them so in the common notion,) there must be great diversity of opinions, and proportionately differing practices.'[17]

Richard Baxter was probably representative of the majority of those who were ejected from the Church of England by the provisions of the Act of Uniformity in 1662. Like them, he had received Episcopal ordination and had no objection in principle to the use of liturgy in worship. What was found obnoxious was the implication that liturgical practices, which most agreed had no absolute divine authority, should be made conditions of Christian fellowship. Thomas Manton probably spoke for them all when he said, 'that which we detest is that the traditions of men should be made equal in dignity and authority with the express revelation of God'.[18] Richard Baxter was a passionate advocate of Christian unity. He wrote, 'we are of one religion for all our differences: [he who] would unite the Church in Kings, in Councils, in any human devices will but divide it'.[19] A later associate of these men was John Howe, who had not received Episcopal ordination. To submit to reordination was an inconsistency that would cast doubt on the validity of his earlier ministry. Seth Ward, Bishop of Exeter, tried to persuade him to conform by accepting reordination. '"Why, pray Sir," said the Bishop to him, "what hurt is there in being twice Ordain'd?" "*Hurt*, my Lord," says *Mr Howe* to him; "the Thought is shocking; it hurts my Understanding; it is an absurdity; For nothing can have two Beginnings."'[20]

Baxter, Manton and Howe were representatives of a group who before the Civil Wars were described as Nonconformists. One result of the Great Ejection of 1662 was to cast them into the company of men who for many years had been members of churches outside the state system and had become known as Separatists. For the Nonconformists, this was a bitter pill to swallow. They were lumped with the Separatists and together this body of ministers and their supporters outside the Church of England became known as Dissenters, until somewhat later all became known as Nonconformists.

It is sometimes suggested that Independent Dissent would not have survived without this massive injection of Presbyterians, with their aristocratic and landed gentry support-ers. I would suggest that it is a remarkable thing that there was a substantial body of Independent Dissenters, Baptist as well as Paedobaptist, with whom the Presbyterians could join forces. How do we explain this? We need to take account of something that happened long before. Let me quote from a lecture deliv-ered by Professor David Daniell in September 1995:

> What had happened to England between 1526 (the date of Tyndale's first New Testament) and 1553 when Mary came to the throne was that the Bible in English had arrived, and had been read, massively, usually in small groups of lay men and women. That was William Tyndale's doing. Not to understand the massivity of that change among the laity is to get that period wrong, I am convinced. Again and again we meet, in John Foxe and elsewhere, some church official's astonishment at the thoroughness of the Bible knowledge of often the humblest men and women: men and women, I add who often could not read, a telling power of the thorough-ness of these 'conventicles' or whatever.[21]

This is of course only half of the story. These biblically literate Christians responded to preachers who believed that churches should be ordered by the Word of God. The best of them were not however interested in ecclesiology as an end in itself. At their best they were represented by men like William Ames who believed that 'theology is the doctrine of living to God' and that living to God can best be sustained in fellowship with churches which are subservient to the kingship of Christ.

Chapter 3

The Nonconformist Minister

Stuart Olyott

True Nonconformity is the fruit of a spiritual experience. If you fail to understand this, you will misunderstand Nonconformity completely. You will never understand Wyclif and the Lollards. You will never grasp why John Hooper made such a fuss about ecclesiastical vestments in the 1550s. You will never be able to make sense of the deep and increasing unease experienced by Puritans in the national church during the years 1560-1660. You will be baffled as to why the oh-so-conciliatory Richard Baxter was the very first clergyman to decline the terms of the Act of Uniformity of 1662. And how will you ever be able to explain why John Bunyan went to prison, or why Philip Doddridge consecrated his massive learning outside the universities? True Nonconformity is the fruit of a spiritual experience. The failure to take this on board is the principal reason why so many Christian people still fail to understand why some of us remain Nonconformists today.

Just as people become Christians one at a time, so they become Nonconformists one at a time. God's Word and Spirit combine together to carry into the very *soul* of a person a conviction which both fires and controls them.

What is that conviction? It is simply this: in the Christian life it is sometimes necessary to lose out. You may have to lose your reputation, your influence, your usefulness, your job, your health, your family, your friends, your freedom or anything else that you value. You may even have to lose your life. But there is one thing that must *never* be lost, and there is never any need for you to do so. That one thing is a clear conscience before God. It is this conviction, all on its own, that drives Nonconformity. This fact explains why Nonconformists throughout their history have fought continuously for freedom of conscience.

How can you keep a conscience like that? There is only one way: it is to *believe* all that God in his Word requires you to believe (orthodoxy) and to *do* all that God in his Word requires you to do (orthopraxy).

Orthopraxy is required in all areas of our life. It is not just a question of obeying God's Word in our personal behaviour. It also requires us to do his revealed will in our families, in society and in our churches — including activities, structures, ministry, discipline and ways of doing things. Believing this is what compelled Hooper to make his famous cry, 'Let the Primitive Church be restored!' Believing this is what moved almost two thousand godly ministers to leave the national church in the Great Ejection of 1662.

Those who are not Nonconformists seldom manage to grasp that Nonconformity is a matter of the *heart*. I can illustrate this by a conversation that I once had on the pavement outside the buildings of Belvidere Road church in Toxteth, Liverpool, where I was privileged to be the pastor for twenty-three years. I was standing at a point from which our buildings looked particularly huge, when along came an Anglican minister whose parish church had just been knocked down and replaced by something very much smaller. He was a godly man and a personal friend, but I sensed that he was somewhat peeved that our buildings were now much larger and more imposing than his. Our conversation quickly turned to the subject of ecclesiology, and as to why he was an Anglican while I was a Nonconformist. Eventually he said something like this: 'Well, I suppose, at the end of the day, it is a matter of temperament. We are very different from each other. You are just not suited for Anglicanism, just as I would never fit in a free church'.

However, my friend should have recognized that, if I had so decided, I would have made a very good Anglican indeed! Although I am half Welsh, I studied at an English Public School that was an Anglican foundation. It was there that I picked up a reasonably Anglican voice that I have never been able to shake off. I have a fair knowledge of Anglican liturgy, and even a measure of affection for it. I have often sung as a chorister in an Anglican cathedral. To this day, I love what is usually called 'church music'. I am not short of friends within the Anglican communion, some of whom are quite highly placed there. On finishing my formal theological studies, it would not have been hard for me to take the appropriate steps towards Anglican ordination. Believe me, if I could be an Anglican, I would be. In my case I can say quite categorically that being a Nonconformist is nothing to do with temperament.

It is all to do with conscience. Inside the Nonconformist heart is a voice crying, 'Woe!' It is the voice crying, 'Woe is me if I do not preach the gospel!' (1 Cor. 9:16), a voice, which, of course, cries out in many Anglican hearts as well. What is different is that in the Nonconformist heart the voice also cries, 'Woe is me if my gospel-preaching *church* does not please him at every point!' And so it is that even if every Anglican congregation in the world was composed of believers proclaiming the gospel of Christ, in spite of our sincere rejoicing at that fact, countless numbers of us would still have to remain Nonconformists. Our consciences do not allow us to follow any other route.

However, my briefing in this chapter is not to talk about Nonconformity at large, but to consider the Nonconformist minister. I have been asked to do this without making any reference to his *preaching*, so as not to overlap with anything that Geoff Thomas will say. Quite frankly, this is like being asked to fly an aeroplane without any wings! In this chapter, then, we will only be free to taxi around the airport. Geoff Thomas will put the wings on later, and then we shall fly!

How, then, shall we proceed? In presenting my material I am going to rely quite heavily on what has been written by someone else. There is no point in trying to re-invent the wheel. It is legitimate, however, to keep the shape of your cartwheel, while giving it metal spokes and hubs, and pneumatic tyres. Good material from previous days does not have to re-appear in an outdated format.

The order of my comments has been inspired by an extended essay entitled 'The Apostolic Church', written by Thomas Witherow in 1856[1]. So who was he? His life spanned the years 1824-1890. He was a Presbyterian minister in Northern Ireland, where he became Professor of church history in Londonderry. He was a Presbyterian and I am an Independent, but because we have so much in common we can hold hands as I address the subject before us. As I follow him closely, but not slavishly, I wish to draw your attention to eight statements, which, because of space, I will not be able to explore fully. These will be followed by four conclusions.

Eight statements

1. Churches are societies of Christians

You cannot talk about ministers without quickly using the word 'church'. How does the New Testament use this word? Today, as in history, it is used in a whole variety of ways. For example, people use it to speak about a building, or a group of people meeting in a building, or a particular denomination, or as a term referring to all Christians in the world. The New Testament knows nothing of the word 'church' being used in these ways. In Scripture the word has only one main meaning. It means *an assembly of the people of God, a society of Christians.*

This is not hard to prove. It is enough to take down a concordance and to look up every occurrence of the word 'church' in the Scriptures. Apart from two occasions where it refers to the gathering of the nation of Israel in Old Testament times, you will not experience any embarrassment at any point if you simply replace the word 'church' by the phrase 'society of Christians'.

So in Colossians 4:15 the apostle Paul writes, 'Greet the brethren who are in Laodicea, and Nymphas and the church that is in his house'[2]. Here the word 'church' refers to a *society of Christians* small enough to meet in a private house.

Acts 11:22, however, reads as follows: 'Then news of these things came to the ears of the church in Jerusalem...'. In this instance the word 'church' refers to a *society of Christians*, possibly numbering thousands of people, all of whom were living in the same city.

1 Corinthians 12:28 refers to the *society of Christians* who were living on earth at the time. It reads, 'And God has appointed these in the church: first apostles, second prophets, third teachers, after that miracles, then gifts of healings, helps, administrations, varieties of tongues.'

Ephesians 5:25 refers to the *society of Christians* in the very largest sense. It is a verse about all those for whom Christ died, the whole family of God, the total number of saints in heaven and on earth. Is your heart not moved when you read, 'Christ ... loved the church and gave himself for it'?

Of course, these verses provide only a representative sample of the data available to us in the New Testament. But who can dispute that on each occasion the word 'church' carries the same meaning? It is true that you have to look at the immediate context to work out whether the writer has in mind a small group, a city-wide community, all Christians on earth, or the total number of the elect. But the fact remains that 'church' as a word has only one principal meaning, although it has such a variety of applications.

This subject needs more than the hurried attention we have just given to it. Its interest for us in this particular chapter lies in this: when *we* use the word 'church' we are not referring to a body made up of Christians and non-Christians. We are referring always and without exception to a *society made up of true Christians only*.

This conviction is foundational to Nonconformity. Our forefathers put it this way: 'Those ... called (through the Ministry of the Word by his Spirit) he commandeth to walk together in particular Societies or Churches...'[3]. If unconverted people manage to slip into such churches, it is because we cannot read anyone's heart, and their profession of faith seems to us to be credible. But they are *not* members of Christ's church. This is why people whose profession of faith ceases to be credible are removed from the membership of *every* true Nonconformist church.

However, in these societies of Christians on earth, there are some members who rule while there are others who obey. In other words, there are officers and private members. This is clear from such verses as 1 Thessalonians 5:12-13 and Hebrews 13:17. The first of these says, 'And we urge you, brethren, to recognize those who labour among you, and are over you in the Lord and admonish you, and to esteem them very highly in love for their work's sake.' The second says, 'Obey those who rule over you, and be submissive, for they watch out for your souls, as those who must give account. Let them do so with joy and not with grief, for that would be unprofitable for you.' With such verses as these in their minds, our forefathers wrote: 'A particular Church gathered and compleated according to the minde of Christ, consists of Officers and Members...'[4]

There is, then, some form of *government* in the church. But we all know that government cannot be abstract or invisible. By its very nature it assumes a *form.*

There is sufficient material in the New Testament for us to discover Christ's will relating to the form of government which is to prevail in his church. This material is not presented methodically, nor does it give to us all the fine detail that we hanker after. But the material is *there,* and the principles of church government which it unveils are clear.

This being so, we should not ignore that material, as so many have done in the past, and as so many continue to do in the present. Nor should we adopt patterns of church government and ministry, and *then* try to justify them from Scripture (an approach so often used in history). Instead, we should discern from the Scriptures what the Lord expects of us, and then set out to put *that* into practice. This is the approach adopted by the Puritans in the period 1560-1660, and it is the approach used by all true Nonconformists ever since.

If we adopt such an approach, what we do we come up with? This is the Nonconformist quest, and it leads us directly into the second of our eight statements.

2. Churches are societies of Christians in which there are but two continuing offices

A quick reading through the New Testament reveals that in the early church there were many offices, namely, apostles, prophets, evangelists, overseers (also known as elders, or pastors and teachers) and deacons. The order in which I have listed them is important. My own personal conviction is that each of these officers had the right to exercise all the offices below him on the list, but that no one had the right to exercise any office above him. Each superior office included all below it.

Some of these offices were temporary; they were necessary during the early days of Christianity, but were not necessary for ever afterwards.

Apostles were men who had seen the Lord Jesus Christ physically after his resurrection, who were specifically appointed by him to be infallible teachers of the gospel and founders of the Christian church, who were able to work miracles that would authenticate their position, and who could lay hands on others for them to receive the Holy Spirit. Having served the purpose for which the Lord sent them, they disappeared from the world and have left no successors.

Prophets were receivers and transmitters of divine revelation. They were necessary because the New Testament church, being the new covenant community, could not live *only* on the Scriptures that had been given during the old covenant period. Prophets continued in the church until God's inscripturated revelation was complete.

Evangelists were men who travelled from place to place preaching the gospel. Most of them were apostolic delegates who spent their time organizing newly-founded churches and defending them from false teachers. Their sphere of duty was not limited to a particular congregation. Their authority extended to the church universal. There is evidence that some of their *functions* continue. Some will argue that this is also true of apostles and prophets, but there is no evidence that such an authority-bearing *office* continues.

The offices of *bishop* and *deacon*, however, were designed to be perpetual in the church. *Bishops* (that is, overseers, also called elders, or pastors and teachers) were office-bearers who were charged to instruct and govern the church. *Deacons* were men who were charged to take upon themselves all eldership responsibilities that were preventing the elders from giving themselves to their prime work. So, for example, they were particularly taken up with temporal concerns such as helping the poor.

As long as the Lord's people have both spiritual and bodily needs, these continuing offices will be necessary. But we must remember that elders and deacons are *congregational* officers whose ministry, for the most part, lies within the bounds of the particular congregation that they have been appointed to serve.

Nonconformists, with very few exceptions, agree that the position that I have just outlined is biblical[5]. Because of the way that God has dealt with them (as outlined in my introduction to this chapter) and the way that their conscience is thus bound to the Word of God, this is the position that they consider themselves called to uphold and practise.

3. These officers are chosen from among the people, by the people

The time came when our Lord Jesus Christ ascended into heaven. From that time on, with the single exception of Paul (who, as he puts it, was 'born out of due time'[6]), men were no longer put into office by the voice of the living Lord. So how were they appointed? Let us look at three examples.

Acts 1:13-26 tells us how Matthias came to occupy the vacancy left in the list of the apostles by the death of Judas Iscariot. Peter addresses the 120 disciples, reminds them of the vacancy and states the qualifications necessary for whoever may fill it. The 120 disciples propose two candidates, but how are they to know which one of them is the right choice? The issue is decided by a time of church prayer and the casting of lots.

So, although Peter was very active in the process, the appointment of the person did not rest with him, but with the *people*. And so it was that Matthias became a minister (v. 26), bishop (v. 20b, *episkopen* in Greek) and apostle (vv. 25-26).

Acts 14:23, our second example, tells us how Barnabas and Paul ordained elders in the new churches of Galatia. If we are reading the Authorized Version, or the New King James Version, it is easy to misunderstand this verse. In the NKJV it reads, 'So when they had appointed elders in every church, and prayed with fasting, they commended them to the Lord in whom they had believed.' But who, precisely, are the 'they' who 'appointed elders'? The Greek verb used here means 'to elect by a show of hands', a fact which, I believe, is now more or less admitted by scholars everywhere.

What happened, then, is that Barnabas and Paul organized the whole process. They may even have made, or vetoed, the nominations. But it was the *people themselves* who elected their elders.

Our third example comes from Acts 6:1-7. Here the apostles, serving as elders of the Jerusalem congregation, are suffering from the pressure of work. They are finding it impossible to give themselves 'continually to prayer and to the ministry of the word' (v. 4), which is, after all, what they have been called to do above everything else. But do *they* appoint the men on whom they are going to devolve the responsibility of caring for the temporal needs of the congregation? No! Instead they set a precedent which all succeeding generations will find easy to follow.

What they do is this: they explain their predicament, spell out the qualifications, ask the congregation to find such men, and promise to give themselves to their first work. The seven men chosen by the *people* were the first deacons — the text does not say so expressly, but almost everyone is agreed that this was the case. Yes, the lowest office-bearer in the early church was chosen from among the people, by the people.

Christ's will for his church is that office-bearers should come into office by popular election!

> The way appointed by Christ for the calling of any
> person, fitted and gifted by the Holy Ghost, unto the
> Office of Pastor, Teacher or Elder in a Church, is, that
> he be chosen thereunto by the common suffrage of the
> Church itself, and solemnly set apart by Fasting and
> Prayer, with Imposition of Hands of the Eldership of that
> Church, if there be any before constituted therein: And
> of a Deacon, that he be chosen by the like suffrage, and
> set apart by Prayer, and the like Imposition of Hands[7].

'After having taken all due care to choose one for the work of
the ministry, they are, by and with the unanimous consent or
suffrage of the church, to proceed to his ordination.'[8]

As popular election of officers is Christ's declared will, it is a
Nonconformist conviction that every other means of appointment is defective, and may even be illegitimate.

4. The offices of bishop and elder are identical

This is a point that we have been taking for granted. The time
has now come for us to establish it.

If you were reading through the New Testament for the first
time, there is something you could not fail to notice: there is
no verse anywhere which speaks of bishops *and* elders, as if
they were two distinct offices. For example, in Philippians 1:1,
the apostle Paul mentions 'the bishops and deacons', but says
nothing of elders. In James 5:14, however, the writer tells ill
people to 'call for the elders of the church', but says nothing of
bishops.

How are we to explain this? And why are bishops and elders
not ever mentioned as two distinct offices? A second reading of
the New Testament would quickly give us the answer: the two
offices are identical!

Titus 1:5-7 proves this. After telling Titus that he must 'appoint elders in every city as I commanded you' (v. 5), Paul pro-
ceeds to say, 'for a *bishop* must be blameless, as a steward of
God...' (v. 7). In talking of elders, Paul was talking of bishops.
The two offices are identical.

The point is made equally clearly in Acts 20:17 and 28. 'From Miletus [Paul] sent to Ephesus and called for the elders of the church' (v. 17). One of the things that he said to them was, 'Take heed to yourselves and to all the flock, among which the Holy Spirit has made you *overseers...*' (v. 28). The word here translated 'overseers' (Greek: *episkopous*) is the word which is normally translated 'bishops'. Elders are bishops, and bishops are elders.

If these two examples were not enough to convince us, the matter, surely, would be clinched by 1 Peter 5:1-4. Peter's address is to 'the elders who are among you' (v. 1), whose responsibilities include 'serving as *overseers*' (v. 2). As we have just seen, 'overseers' are bishops. But the passage declares that it is elders who fulfil this office. This can only be because the offices of bishop and elder are identical.

When we understand this, a passage like 1 Timothy 3:1-13 makes immediate sense. Here we have the qualifications of bishops listed immediately before those of deacons. Timothy had been sent by Paul to sort out some problems in the church of Ephesus. There was no hope of this happening if the wrong sort of men were in office. But the only offices envisaged by the apostle were those of bishop (v. 1) and deacon (v. 8). This fits in exactly with what we have discovered about elders and deacons being the only continuing offices in the church.

There is, however, something else that it is important for us to notice. Bishops, that is, elders, are also *pastors*. For example, the elders/overseers/bishops of 1 Peter 5:1-4 are told to 'shepherd the flock of God' (v. 2). The verse could be just as correctly translated, '*Pastor* the flock of God'. In the same way, in Acts 20:28 Paul instructs the elders/overseers/bishops of Ephesus to 'shepherd (or *pastor*) the church of God which he purchased with his own blood.'

In those two examples it is a verb (to *shepherd/pastor*) that is used. However, in Ephesians 4:11-16 the apostle Paul uses a noun. We have already looked briefly at these verses. Among the men that Christ has given to serve his church are 'pastors and teachers' (v. 11). Almost everyone agrees that Paul is not talking about two sorts of men here, but one. Perhaps in more modern English we should call such a man a pastor-teacher. But that is not our main focus of interest here. Rather, we are forced to ask the question, 'Why in the other examples do the Scriptures tell all elders/overseers/bishops "to pastor", using a verb, while on this occasion it is the noun "pastor-teacher" that is used?' The answer probably lies along lines like these: whereas most elders supported themselves financially by means of their daily work, some elders gave themselves to their work in such a way that they had to renounce their former calling, live by the gospel, and be supported by the churches that they served. To do this they needed a level of 'calling' and conviction that the other elders, by the very nature of things, did not need to share. So while all elders were called by the Lord 'to pastor' (verb), the men specially set aside for this work were known as 'pastors' (noun).

Not all Nonconformists, and certainly not all readers, will agree with the second half of the previous paragraph. But the Scriptural evidence for everything else included under this fourth statement is clear and unambiguous: there is a continuing office in Christ's church called *elder*. Those who occupy that office are called to *shepherd/pastor* the flock (by feeding the sheep with the Word) and are also *bishops/overseers* (directing and ruling that flock by the same Word). By means of his Word, our Lord Jesus Christ has revealed this so clearly that we have to conclude that any system of church government not submitting to this truth is a direct challenge to his authority.

5. In each church there is to be a plurality of elders

As far as I know, this conviction is rooted in every Nonconformist heart, although it is not always worked out 'on the ground' in exactly the same way. Some take this principle to mean that there should be a plurality of elders in each *congregation*. Others see it differently. They argue, for example, that some of the churches of the New Testament (like those of Jerusalem and later of Rome) probably had thousands of members. In the absence of church buildings (which, of course, did not become common until the fourth century) it was just not possible that all the members of a large church could all have gathered in the same place at the same time. So, although there was a plurality of elders in *every church*, there was not necessarily more than one elder present in *every* one of the groups, or *congregations*, making up that church.

These two ways of expressing a commonly held principle can be seen in history. A given Nonconformist church, meeting in a building in a given street, may have a plurality of elders and, if necessary, a number of deacons as well. Around the corner, however, is another Nonconformist church whose only officers are 'the pastor' and 'the deacons'. If pressed to justify their respective practices, the first church would argue that the principle of the plurality of elders should be applied in the first way outlined above. This is because it believes the equation *congregation=church*. The second church would argue that the principle should be applied in the second way outlined above. This is because it believes the equation *congregation=a group within the church in that community*. I need to say, however, that my personal observation is that those who hold to the first application generally argue their case much more robustly, and with much more appeal to Scripture, than those who hold to the second — with glorious exceptions, of course!

Whatever our differences may be over the application of the principle, I must underline that consistent Nonconformists are not divided over the truth of the principle itself. We hold to it because we believe that the Word of God teaches it. In Acts 14:23 we read that 'they ... appointed elders in *every* church.' In Acts 20:17 and 28 the important nouns are in the plural: '[Paul] sent to Ephesus and called for the elders of the church ... "Take heed to yourselves and to all the flock among which the Holy Spirit has made you overseers"'. In Philippians 1:1 the apostle Paul describes that local church as being composed of 'all the saints in Christ Jesus who are in Philippi, with the bishops and deacons'. The plural is found again in Paul instructions to Titus in Titus 1:5: 'Appoint elders in *every* city as I commanded you.'

There are other passages in the New Testament addressed to elders in the plural, but, surely, these four examples alone are enough to settle the question. In the light of them, who can resist the conclusion that in New Testament days there was in *each* church a *plurality* of elders? This, of course, is the same as saying that in *each* church there was a *plurality* of bishops! It is in this way that our Lord Jesus Christ has revealed his will for all churches of all succeeding generations.

6. Ordination to office is done corporately

In the New Testament quite a lot is said about 'the laying on of hands'. This sometimes occurs when spiritual gifts are being conferred[9] or when ill people are being miraculously healed[10]. It also occurs when men are being solemnly set aside for ministry, even though *no* miraculous gifts may be being conferred — which suggests that formal ordination is something that should continue even when miraculous gifts have been withdrawn.

Apostles, of course, ordained men to office, as did their delegates. But, as we have seen, neither apostles nor their delegates exist today, and so their functions cannot provide us with a pattern of church life. So how should ordination be done in the post-apostolic church?

Three texts will help us here. In 1 Timothy 4:14 we are told that Timothy was formally set aside for the ministry, not by an apostle or apostolic delegate, but by 'the laying on of the hands of the presbytery' (that is, the eldership). It was done by the elders in their collective capacity.

Acts 13:1-3 tells us that something similar happened when Barnabas and Saul were commissioned for missionary service. No apostles or apostolic delegates were imported for the occasion. The ordination was done by the Antioch church leaders in their collective capacity.

The ordination of the first deacons, recorded in Acts 6:6, is particularly interesting. It was done by a plurality of leaders, although those leaders were apostles! Corporate ordination was obviously the course of action that the apostles preferred. We must remember that at that time they were acting as church elders — a further confirmation of my personal conviction, outlined earlier, that higher offices include all those below them.

When we put all this data together, what do we see? We see that apostles did not ordain alone when it was possible for them to do it corporately. Where apostles were not present, ordination was done by the existing church leaders acting in a collective capacity. No other authority was expected or required.

We can go no further. In a biblically organized church the elders are the leaders, and it is they, therefore, who should do the ordaining. Some modern Nonconformists have been squeamish about believing and practising this, but this was not the case with most of the early ones. Their position was well summarized by Benjamin Keach: 'After having taken all due care to choose one for the work of the ministry, they are, by and with the unanimous consent or suffrage of the church, to proceed to his ordination: which is a solemn setting apart of such a person for the sacred function, in this wise, by setting apart a day of fasting and prayer, Acts 13:2,3. The whole church being present, he is to have the hands of the presbytery of that church, or of neighbouring elders called and authorized by that church, whereof such a person is a member, solemnly laid upon him, 1 Tim. 5:22, Titus 1:5, Acts 14:23, 1 Tim. 4:14, and thus such a person is to be recommended into the work of the Lord, and to take particular care of the flock of whom he is thus chosen, Acts 20:28'[11].

7. Policy decisions are an eldership responsibility

'Policy decisions' are decisions which govern the whole ethos and direction of the congregation, as opposed to the thousands of small day-to-day decisions which do not affect that ethos and direction at all — who will open the doors next Sunday? Should the thermostat be set at twenty or twenty-one degrees? Should the walls of the entrance hall be painted light blue or pastel green?

The church at Antioch in Syria had a massive policy decision to make: should it receive uncircumcised Gentile believers into its fold, or not? If so, should it consider them as having the same standing as circumcised Jewish believers?

Now Presbyterians and Independents read Acts 15:1-29 in very different ways, but the very least we can say about this incident is this:

a. The Antioch church, by means of its leaders, very naturally consulted the church at Jerusalem, from which its first members had come, from which its first Bible-teacher had come, and from which the people now troubling it had come.

b. The apostles were still at Jerusalem and functioning as elders there (because, as I have contended, higher offices include all those below them). But the Jerusalem church, in addition, now also had a body of elders. It was to *this* body of apostolic elders and newer elders that the policy decision was referred.

c. The discussion of the issue, and the decision relating to it, was made entirely by those apostles-acting-as-elders and the newer elders. The Jerusalem church members consented to it and added their name to it.

The decision-making body at Jerusalem was clearly the eldership. The use of 'bishop' for elder throughout the New Testament also makes it clear that the rule and oversight of the local church is their responsibility. We have seen, however, that elders are plural and that they act corporately. Our seventh statement is thus biblically justified: policy decisions are an eldership responsibility.

8. And yet the only Head of the church is the Lord Jesus Christ

Who can doubt that this is the clear teaching of the New Testament? The Savoy Declaration crystallized it like this: 'By the appointment of the Father all Power for the Calling, Institution, Order, or Government of the Church, is invested in a Supreme and Sovereign manner in the Lord Jesus Christ, as King and Head thereof'[12].

There is nothing in the New Testament that even hints that any earthly ruler (even a Christian one!) has, or could have, by virtue of his position, any authority in the church of Jesus Christ. The teaching everywhere is, rather, that in temporal matters the Christian bows to the laws of the land as administered by even the lowest official, but in spiritual matters he does not even bow to Caesar on his throne.

Nor is spiritual power lodged in the hands of any office-bearer of the church, however godly his character, however great his gifts, and however fruitful his ministry may be. The pattern instead is this:

    a. Christians are commanded to obey those who have the rule over them[13]. We have seen that these are elders.

    b. The elders, however, are commanded not to act as lords over God's heritage, but to be examples to the flock[14].

    c. Even the apostles do not claim to be princes in God's church, but see themselves as fellow-workers for the ordinary Christian's joy[15].

    d. Even Peter does not claim any supremacy over the other apostles. He acts with his fellow-apostles as a simple preacher of the cross. He never nominates anyone to ecclesiastical office. He never pulls rank on any officers lower down the list. Another apostle even withstands him to his face, because he is to be blamed![16]

We can conclude, then, that spiritual authority is not deposited in any earthly ruler, nor is it deposited in any church officer. The church has *no* lawgiver other than the Lord Jesus Christ Himself. He, and *he only*, is 'the head over all things to the church' (Eph. 1:22), the 'head of the church' (Eph. 5:23), 'the head of the body, the church' (Col. 1:18).

Let us be blunt about this: a body cannot have two heads. Nobody can sit on the fence on this issue. If Christ is the Head of the church, then the Pope is not, the Queen is not, nor is any other dignitary (or committee!) ecclesiastical or political. If *any* earthly figure is the head of the church, then Christ is not.

The choice is stark, but real: we must reject the authority of the Bible on this point, or we must accept it and submit to it! Submitting to the headship of Christ means *in practice* submitting to the teaching of the Scriptures, for we have no other way of knowing Christ's mind.

How clearly John Hooper[17] saw this! Let us listen to him:

> The Scriptures are the Law of God; none may set aside their commands nor add to their injunctions. Christ's kingdom is a spiritual one. In this neither pope nor king may govern. Christ alone is the Governor of His Church and the only Lawgiver ... Christ hath given the Scriptures to judge thy bishop, doctor, preacher and curate, whether he preach gall or honey, his own laws or God's laws. The Church of Christ the more it is burdened by men's laws the further it is from the true and sincere verity of God's Word. The Scripture and the Apostles' churches are solely to be followed, and no man's authority, or even cherubim or seraphim[18].

It is simply not true to say (as so many writers do) that no clear form of church government is revealed in the New Testament. What sort of Head of the church would Christ be if he had not revealed what his church was, and how it was to be organized? This, we believe, he *has* revealed, and that his mind can be summed up in the eight statements we have made. It is because we are convinced of the biblical reliability of these statements that we can now draw four conclusions.

Four conclusions

1. We are now in a position to evaluate different ecclesiologies

Prelacy, especially as it manifests itself in a national church, falls at every point. Prelacy is that system of church government that is characterized by a hierarchy of individuals — for example, archbishops, bishops, deans, priests, deacons, etc., — fanning down from one individual at the top. The Roman

Catholic Church and the Church of England are both prelatic; Rome vests ecclesiastical supremacy in the Pope, while the Church of England vests it in the reigning monarch. If we compare prelacy point by point with our eight statements, we can see that it is an *entirely* human system and that it has no right to be the system that prevails in *any* body that calls itself a church of Jesus Christ.

Congregationalism falls at several points. Congregationalism is characterized by the autonomy of the local church, and rule being exercised by the congregation through a process of democratic voting to get a consensus. If we compare Congregationalism point by point with our eight statements, we can see that it frequently falls on point five and always falls on point seven. Congregationalists, therefore, may be called 'inconsistent Nonconformists'. We should carefully note that the points on which they fall have serious implications for the Christian ministry.

Most of the early Nonconformists were not Congregationalists. This does not mean, however, that they all fit into neat categories. For example, where would you place Richard Baxter, who was almost willing to be an Episcopalian? And where would you place John Bunyan? He was a Baptist of sorts, but has been called by some 'an unspecified Independent'!

Independency and *Presbyterianism* are both in line with all of our eight statements. Independency is characterised by the autonomy of the local church — this church being ruled by its elders with congregational consent. Presbyterianism is also characterized by the rule of elders at the local level, with congregational consent, but in addition has a gradation of church courts which, in certain circumstances, may give directives to the local congregation.

It is true that Independency and Presbyterianism have some important differences between them, but these differences do not impinge on their essential understanding of the Christian ministry — which is our focus of interest in this chapter. In 1646 John Owen read John Cotton's *The Keys of the Kingdom*, saw the differences between the two systems, and moved from Presbyterianism to Independency. It is interesting to note, however, that his understanding of the nature of the Christian ministry remained unchanged.

I believe that by evaluating varying ecclesiologies in the light of our eight statements, we may conclude that both Independents and Presbyterians may be called 'consistent Nonconformists'.

2. We are now in a position to define what a minister is

He is not a *priest*. The Lord Jesus Christ has done away with the necessity of priests. He alone is our mediator. He alone is our way of access to God. This is clear throughout the New Testament, and especially in the Epistle to the Hebrews.

He is not a *cleric*, someone of a different caste standing in an apostolic succession. Some New Testament churches, such as the one at Colosse, were not founded by the apostles. But these churches do not seem to have lacked a ministry.

He is not an *incumbent*, having some rights over the local church which other members of the congregation do not have. I think that this chapter has already made this repeatedly clear.

So what is he? He is an ordinary Christian man, known for his godly life and the integrity of his family life. He is sound in the faith and able to defend it, has a proven ability to teach the Scriptures, and aspires to the office and work of the ministry.

He is nominated by the existing leadership and elected by the people to serve the local church as one of its elders, but especially to '*labour* in the word and doctrine', as 1 Timothy 5:17 puts it. Wherever possible, he is set aside to give himself entirely to this work, having a right to the financial support of the church that he serves, as the same verse makes clear[19]. It is important to stress, however, that a man can be a legitimate minister without being 'full-time'. A man may need to waive his right to financial support because of the poverty of the people that he serves. You will remember that one of the charges levelled against John Bunyan was that he was a 'mechanik preacher'; in other words, he earned his living by manual labour. But who among us would dare to suggest that John Bunyan was not a legitimate minister of the gospel?

3. We are now in a position to define what a minister's work is

He is a particular sort of elder, doing his work in harness with his fellow elders. Elders are spiritual *shepherds* who feed Christ's flock with his Word, and who, on a spiritual level, do everything else for the sheep that a shepherd would do – nurse them, bind up their wounds, protect and defend them from their enemies, bring them back when they wander, love them, care for them, etc.. They are also *bishops/overseers* under Christ who ensure that his church walks in his ways – that every rule he has given is applied, but that nothing else *whatever* is pressed upon the Christian conscience. This work of ruling will include presiding at meetings, administering the sacraments and implementing restorative discipline. We must recognize, however, that these responsibilities are the province of the *elders*, but not necessarily of the *pastor* (or full-time elder). The New Testament gives us no indication that these responsibilities fall more heavily on the shoulders of one particular man within the eldership.

Wherever possible, the minister does his work full-time, forsaking his previous calling. Quite obviously then, as I have already stressed, he has to have a level of conviction about what he is doing that other elders do not need. Historically this inner conviction, this unquenchable fire in the soul, has been referred to as the 'call to the ministry'. As I have indicated, it is presumably of such men that the noun-form 'pastor' is used, as in Ephesians 4:11, whereas all elders are told *to* pastor, as in Acts 20:28 and 1 Peter 5:2.

Especially where he is full-time, it is likely that the pastor will do the bulk of the teaching that goes on in the church, although the whole eldership is answerable to God for the quality and content of that teaching. This will inevitably mean that he will soon have a higher profile than the other elders and that he will be increasingly both loved and esteemed because of his work. But this fact does not elevate him to a superior rank. Nor must it lead us to conclude that policy decisions are in his hands alone; these clearly remain the responsibility of the whole eldership.

The authority given by Christ to elders, both in teaching and ruling, is to be taken very seriously. And yet we must continue to stress that each of the elders remains himself a member of the flock, and not something 'other' or distinct from it. The language of Scripture is very careful. It tells us that elders are among the flock[20] and that the flock is among them[21]. We are often tempted to think that church members are like private soldiers, while the deacons are corporals, the elders are sergeants, and the minister (i.e. the full-time elder) is an officer! It seems to me that a little bit of Anglicanism often continues to live on in many of us. We do not seem able to avoid thinking of church structures in hierarchical terms. But we must. Obedience to Christ requires it.

4. Finally, we are now in a position to define how *a minister should do his work*

He should do it *humbly*. He is not a prince in the church, nor a priest, cleric or incumbent. He is just an ordinary Christian man who owes all his graces, his gifts and his calling to the Head of the church, for whom he labours as an under-shepherd. What has he got to boast about?

He should do it *incarnationally*. His commission is to be an example to the flock and the embodiment of what he teaches[22]. This is such an important point that the Word of God insists that nearly all the qualifications required of a man aspiring to the ministry are qualities of character[23], with very much less being said about his giftedness, and nothing at all about his academic achievements!

He should do it *conscientiously*. He is answerable to another and will give an account to him of how he has cared for his people's souls. He will be judged more strictly than those he teaches and serves[24]. It was this conviction that was the driving force in the ministry of Richard Baxter. And so it was that he preached twice each Sunday to half the population of Kidderminster, established family worship in hundreds of homes, nurtured his young people, and trained his church members to witness and to pray. He and his assistant also worked closely together to make sure that every family in the parish received two hours of face-to-face catechising at least once a year. Yes, we live in different times. But who can tell what a truly conscientious ministry may yet accomplish?

He should do it *communally*. The Lord has not called him to work alone, and he would therefore be both disobedient and foolish if he tried to do so. He is a member of a team. Although his role is to labour in the Word and doctrine, there is no aspect of his ministry that he is not called on to share with his fellow elders. Even when everything is as bad as it can be, the Lord does not expect him to weep alone. A failure to remember this is one of the chief reasons that good men leave the ministry.

He should do it *prayerfully*. No spiritual work can ever be done without God's blessing. The only certain way for him to know that blessing is to constantly cast himself on the Lord. There are things that get in the way of the minister's prayer life and there are things that get in the way of his studying and preaching the Word. This is also true of the praying and ministering of the other elders. Everything that does this — everything! — must be put into the hands of the deacons. That is why our Lord instituted the diaconate. The greatest priorities must never be neglected.

He should do it *authoritatively*. He did not take this great work upon himself. Christ called him to do it. This call was recognized and confirmed by the local church. Now he expounds Christ's Word and binds every conscience to Christ's instructions. How could such a ministry be less than authoritative?

He should do it *firmly*. He is to insist that the church is run at every point according to the revealed will of its Head. Among other things, this means that he will ensure that no one comes into church membership, or remains in it, whose profession of faith is not credible. It also means that he will constantly promote that standard of doctrine and life which Christ expects of his churches, and will enforce it by admonition, suspension or exclusion, depending on which step of restorative discipline is appropriate in each particular case. Such firmness has often been exemplified in history. Out of the thousands who sat under his ministry, Richard Baxter would allow only six hundred to attend communion. And how can we forget Jonathan Edwards's great and costly stand on the same issue?

He should do it *gently*. He is to constantly recall that the people who make up his church are Christ's sheep, not his own. He will always treat them as such. Each one — boy, girl, teenager, man, woman, older person — is precious, and so is to be cared for, nurtured, fed, healed, sought or restored, but never lorded over.

He should do it *sacrificially*. The shepherd must be willing to give his own life, or to make any other necessary sacrifice *whatever*, for the good of the sheep. If he does not have this willingness, it will prove that he is nothing but a hired hand whose principal reason for being in the ministry is his own advantage[25]. The shepherd exists for the sheep; the sheep do not exist for the shepherd. So who is this man who does not spare himself in the work of the ministry although fifty years of his life are spent in chronic ill health? Who is he who, for over twenty years from 1662, risks fines and imprisonment so that he can preach to his people and meet their spiritual needs? Indeed, during that period he goes to prison twice, once for a week, and once for nearly two years. It is the man who understands better than most men what the work of the ministry involves: Richard Baxter.

* * *

On this note we come to the end of this modest chapter on the Nonconformist minister. Will you not thank the Lord for *every* minister you know of, past or present, who has conformed to, or who today conforms to, the biblical pattern? Conformists like that are *Non*conformist ministers indeed!

Can such ministers be manufactured? No, of course not. The Lord himself must raise them up. And if he does not, what will happen? Such ministers will disappear from the earth. This is a fact that we must not dumb down. Such institutions as the

John Owen Centre at the London Theological Seminary can certainly help the men whom Christ gives to his church, but they cannot create them.

Is it not then time to earnestly petition the Lord of the harvest[26], the Head of the church, that he may show us favour by giving to us the ministers that his churches so desperately need at this hour? Must Mr Valiant-for-Truth disappear from the land? If he does, our churches will collapse in the face of the combined and advancing forces of secularism, consumerism, false religions, demonic 'spiritualities', ecclesiastical anarchy, theological pluralism, confident but diminishing Catholicism, resurgent but confusing Anglicanism, and every other form of error, disobedience and worldliness that threatens us at the moment.

We need a whole new army of Nonconformist ministers! Without such men of God, the cause could be lost! Who will pray with constant and untiring urgency that the Lord will give to us a multitude of ministers after his own heart?

Chapter 4

Nonconformist Preaching
(Dr Lloyd-Jones Memorial Lecture 2004)

Geoffrey Thomas

There is a tradition of Anglican preaching which any Nonconformist would envy. Esteemed men of God, vitally expounding Scripture, have been addressing England from Anglican pulpits since the Reformation: Perkins in the sixteenth century, Gurnall in the seventeenth century, Whitefield in the eighteenth century, while in the nineteenth century there was the incomparable Ryle. In the twentieth century, Alec Motyer has been one of those Anglicans who has never failed to help us each time we have heard him preach. Such men are simply the representatives of gospel preachers who have brought the Word of God to bear upon the Church of England since the Reformation. Our unity with all the elect of God who cleave to the historic faith has been experienced as we have listened to these Anglican brethren preaching from the Bible and applying its truth to us. Some of the Anglican choice of music is as deplorable as ever — they have travelled from choir boys to rock bands and have not stopped yet. One waits for the drummer to lay down his sticks and then the sermon can begin. To our delight in the sermon we are shown Jesus Christ's glory, sin is made shameful, and grace magnified as more abundant than all our guilt. At such times we have forgotten the less important convictions that divide Anglicanism and Nonconformity. It is in biblical preaching that we are of most assistance and encouragement to one another, Free Churchmen and Established

Churchmen who have been saved by the precious blood of Christ who love to proclaim the Bible.

The Church of England gives its incumbents a protection and an almost unchallenged authority within its pulpits (at which our Nonconformist preachers spectate and marvel), but accepting the Establishment status can also discourage the preaching of the whole counsel of God except amongst its most courageous clergy. To keep one's conscience clear and remain an evangelical vicar means a life of constant vigilance and Christian warfare. If our supreme loyalty is to Jesus Christ, we may not view every fellow clergyman who has been the recipient of Episcopal ordination as a brother. The recent 180-page report *Fragmented Faith?*, coming jointly from the practical theology department of Bangor University and the *Church Times*, indicates how much humanism has infringed upon the Christian faith in the Anglican denomination. One in thirty-three clerics doubts the existence of God. If reflected throughout the church's nine thousand clergy, the finding would mean that nearly three hundred Church of England clergy are uncertain that God exists. Forty per cent of clergy do not believe in the virgin birth of Christ; a third of clergy are in favour of the ordination of practising homosexuals and homosexual bishops. Over half the clergy do not think it is wrong for people of the same gender to have sex together. We may not ignore the warnings of Jesus concerning false prophets. Our consciences may not be bought by the smiling greetings in 'ministers' mingles' and clergy conferences of those who preach another gospel. Fearlessness and vigilance is the price to pay for being a gospel-preaching vicar in the twenty-first century, as it always has been.

That vigilance is often absent. Evangelicalism in the Church of England is overwhelmingly Arminian and charismatic, and its preaching reflects those inadequate theological systems. The appeal of those sermons is directed to the congregation's will in order, firstly, to get men to make a decision for God, and, secondly, to decide to speak or sing in tongues. Feelings and physical manifestations are judged to be of considerable importance, while the fact is that they are the easiest manifestations for the devil to counterfeit. Its music, rather than the preached Word, creates the tone of that worship, and the emotional responses of the congregation are interpreted authoritatively by its leaders in personal pastoring as indicating the presence of saving faith in favoured people and also as evidence of possessing the fulness of the Holy Spirit. Thus assurance is bestowed by clerical pontification.

Anglicanism's best representatives are unhappy with this approach. They take Scripture more seriously, though they are generally Amyraldian and there is always one's uncertainty concerning their belief in Jesus' teaching of the eternal punishment of the unrepentant. Their message focuses upon the importance of exegetical preaching, especially as viewed through the insights of the history of redemption school. Compared to what is heard in many pulpits today this is an important emphasis, but there tends to be a lack of application; there is also the denigration of systematic theology and coolness towards creationism. The goal of the sermon is considered to be explaining what a passage means. Some hearers feel that, if this is so, they could gain as much benefit from staying at home and reading a commentary on that passage. The absence of deep feeling while hearing the truth of the Word preached is compensated for by a cultivated spirit of friendly informality and modest approachability. This is one consequence of the absence of the Calvinistic vision of God-centredness in creation, judgement, redemption and regeneration. However, all the above characteristics are also found in abundance in Nonconformist circles.

We Free Churchmen understand our principal calling to be preaching and pastoring. Hence our status is the preacher or the pastor; we know nothing of such titles as archbishops, diocesan bishops, deans and rural deans, prebendaries, canons and minor canons, priests and fathers, vicar generals and clerks in holy orders. These are to us the baggage of a partially reformed church, offices which Christ never appointed and of which there is nothing at all in the New Testament. How much better the professing church would be without such clutter. We pastor and so we are pastors. We preach and so we are preachers.

Again, Nonconformist preachers are appointed by the call of a particular church. Thus a congregation may maintain its own biblical convictions. New Park Street church did so from Gill to Spurgeon. The congregation called Calvinistic preacher-pastors for a couple of centuries. Gospel congregations have wisdom enough to evaluate a man who claims he is called of God. It will ask questions about Christian doctrine and morality. Does he have a strong call that he must preach the Word of God? Does he feel that he is more than an elder who teaches the Word? Who are the role models of this man? What books has he read which have impacted him? What does he think of Luther, Spurgeon, Lloyd-Jones and their sermons? Does he make an altar call? Does he believe in expository preaching? What is his view of music in worship? Such friendly questioning will seek to discover if there is an agenda of which none of the references they have sought after have even hinted, a package that a man might bring like a Trojan horse into a congregation.

When they have called a man, a relationship develops as the years pass. Affection builds up between a congregation and its pastor. The church speaks with warmth of the one who brings them the Word of God each week and visits them in their need. He might be referred to as 'the Doctor', or some such familiar name of respectful endearment. That affection is contagious and other people know that the bonds that unite that pulpit and those pews are not only the bonds of truth but also love.

Nonconformist churches are characterized by their emphasis on the Word of God rather than on the sacraments. Even the design of their buildings indicates this. The pulpit is central; let everyone see and hear the Bible being read and preached. In some churches the sacrament is held twice a year, or four times a year and at the most twelve times a year. The congregation is utterly satisfied with the grace of God that comes to them morning and evening through the public means of grace. The summit of Nonconformist worship is the preacher doing what the Lord Jesus Christ did in the synagogue in Galilee. He opened the book and found the place. We have spoken to God in prayer, we have sung his praises, and then the climactic aspect of worship is when God speaks to us through his Word. What then is good Nonconformist preaching?

Sermons that are a true proclamation

First it is true proclamation. It is not a string of stories or a stodgy lecture but from first to last the sermon is directed to every hearer. We are all involved from the outset in the herald bringing his king's message to us. The truth of a passage of the Bible is presented not simply as words that once came to members of a church long ago and far away in biblical times, but God becoming significant to us now, saving, ruling, directing, comforting, rebuking, caring and living for us in and by his own Word.

In the eighteenth century, John Nelson records his first encounter with a sermon that was a true proclamation. He heard John Wesley preaching for the first time at Moorfields in London: 'O that was a blessed morning to my soul! As soon as he got upon the stand he stroked back his hair and turned his gaze towards where I stood, and I thought fixed his eyes upon me. His countenance struck such an awful dread upon me before I heard him speak that it made my heart beat like the pendulum of a clock. When he did speak, I thought his whole discourse was aimed at me.'

For a while Nelson fought against those convictions until he heard a soldier testifying to some women how he had become a Christian hearing Wesley: 'When he began to speak his words made me tremble. I thought he spoke to no one but me, and I durst not look up, for I imagined all the people were looking at me.' Nelson sought out Wesley and heard him preach again, finally saying, 'I found power to believe that Jesus Christ had shed his blood for me, and that God, for his sake, had forgiven my offences. Then was my heart filled with love to God and man.' Soon, Nelson became one of Wesley's first assistant ministers, accompanying him to preach in Cornwall and elsewhere. He too became a mighty proclaimer of the divine message of the gospel.

Sermons that are biblical

Secondly, good Nonconformist preaching is biblical preaching. What is preached is not an essay on some truth or the actions of politicians, media personalities, philosophers, theologians or our own opinions on current affairs, but what God has said in one of the letters of Paul, or in one of the books of Moses, or by one of the writing prophets, or in the words of Jesus Christ his only begotten Son. Not only are we told what the portion preached on means, but we are also shown that every point that is made comes from the passage before us. Because this is done we can evaluate for ourselves whether the preacher's conclusions and applications are accurate and thus faithful to the Word. Has he done his homework? The preacher has to satisfy his hearers that he has taught just what that particular passage is saying. We return home understanding the passage, how everything in the sermon flowed from those words that were announced at the beginning. Then we listen to his exhortations about our lives carefully, not as the opinions of one eloquent man, but as the Word of God to us. God's servant preaches and his preaching is received with an authority appropriate for that message. We leave knowing we have heard a proclamation from God to us. Having told us what the passage was, it makes sense to us and others in the congregation. Thus we are all drawn into the speaking God himself. We become a divinely involved people. The Bible becomes the principal means of grace whereby God changes people who receive his Word.

Let me apply some famous words of John Jewel: are you a member of the Royal family? Go and hear the Scriptures preached. Are you sleeping in cardboard city? Go and hear the Scriptures preached. Are you a minister, first hear for yourself the Scriptures being preached. Are you a parent concerned for your children? Then hear the Scriptures preached. Are you a child and concerned about your one lifetime stretching out before you? Then go and hear the Scriptures preached. Are you a rock musician? Then hear the Scriptures preached. Are you a professional footballer? You must make it your goal to go and hear the Scriptures preached. Are you a Muslim? Go and hear the Christian Scriptures preached. Are you planning to become a suicide bomber? First hear the Scriptures being preached. Are you a millionaire? Go and hear Scripture preached. Are you a homosexual? Go and hear the Scriptures preached. Are you a drug addict? Go and hear the Scriptures preached. Are you totally ignorant as to why you are here in the world? Go and hear Scripture preached. Are you dying of cancer? Then send for cassettes of Scripture being preached. Are you proud? Hear the Scriptures preached. Are you in deep trouble? Hear the Scriptures preached. Are you a sinner? Have you offended God? Find a preacher who will preach the Scriptures to you. Are you in despair of the mercy of God? Then hear the Scriptures preached.

Legitimacy for what we believe, the clearest window through which God may be seen, a view of the living Christ, and knowledge of how we must live, is to be found in Scripture and Scripture alone. So all true sermons are biblical sermons.

Sermons that are interesting

Thirdly, Nonconformist preaching is interesting preaching. The juice has not been cooked out of the passage so that it is hard, dry, burnt over, abstract teaching, nor is it raw and bloody, an uncooked chunk of meat. The passage is cooked and garnished and accented so that the many flavours of the Word of God are served by the minister, seasoned by illustrations that he has brought. Thus as the sermon is delivered it sizzles. In the late fifties our family moved to Barry. My father had become the Station Master at Barry Dock and there I discovered an annual Keswick in Wales convention that had been taken over by Omri Jenkins and Paul Tucker. They would preach in the Welsh Congregationalist chapel on the square opposite the town library every year in a week of meetings and both of them would preach each evening. We would sing a hymn; there would be a reading and prayer, another hymn, then either Omri would preach first or Paul Tucker. Then we would sing a hymn and there would be the second sermon afterwards. I do not know whether services with such two sermons exist any longer. Those men were such interesting preachers, fascinating in their personalities and quite gripping in their preaching. Very different kinds of men, it was a privilege to hear them preach.

You can't protest, 'But I have been to the commentaries and I have read the Bible dictionaries, surely you can't ask for anything more?' Yes, we must ask for more. I am asking: should not a family who gathers around a Thanksgiving meal in the U.S.A. get excited as they see the table spread so lovingly? Should not the odour of the prepared food get the saliva ducts working in anticipation of eating such delights, the bowls of steaming peas, the tender turkey, the cranberry sauce, the roast potatoes, the carrots, the jugs of steaming gravy? If a wife returned home with shopping bags loaded with the best food that Sainsbury's provides would not the family rightly complain if she claimed food selection to be everything? 'Don't ask me to prepare and cook and serve it too. You should appreciate the food because it is good, you need it; it constitutes a well-balanced meal.' How would you like it if you returned home for supper tonight and your wife put a Tesco bag on the table and told you, 'Well, you have a go for a change', and there was a cauliflower in cling film, a bag of uncooked rice, a couple of cuts of raw Welsh lamb, some coffee beans in a plastic bag and a box of do-it-yourself chocolate cake. Would you be turned on by that? Could you be strengthened by those bags and packages, even if it were wonderfully nutritious and well-balanced in assortment?

The analogy is not that inappropriate. There are pastors who spend little or no time beyond exegesis in preparing to make the truth of a passage edible, and so God's people go away unfed. The pastor wonders why the people don't grow. The food was there, the combination was fine, but why didn't people eat it? It is not enough to protest, 'If they are hungry, they'll find a way of eating it.' What are they going to do with the uncooked rice and those coffee beans? No matter how nutritious the ingredients of a meal may be, little actual eating will take place with food that is not properly prepared. The preacher is the naked chef. He stands terribly exposed and vulnerable before God, bringing his Word of life to a hundred hungry people. Serve God's truth in a savoury and appetizing way.

It sounds very pious to say you are spending all of your time on exegesis, the history of redemption and hermeneutics, but it is very clear that form and content are really inseparable. Just as the true flavours of meats and vegetables cannot really be appreciated until they are properly cooked, so too there can be no adequate understanding or appreciation of many biblical truths until they are put in a form that is compelling to the hearer. You remember there is bound to be some structure of one kind or another; a sermon begins and a sermon finally ends. So whenever God's Word is preached, form is unavoidable. But wrapped cauliflower on a plate, and ten coffee beans at the bottom of a mug are the worst form for eating. Such form actually distorts. Coffee is to be drunk, not chewed. Our task is to bring out the flavours of each passage and serve the ends which the Holy Spirit, who inspired the passage, had in his heart when he inspired those particular words in that unique combination. Those specific words will give the specific message that comes out of it its own structure. The key to the ensuing form may be just one word.

I remember once at Westminster Chapel, Dr Lloyd-Jones was preaching through the Acts of the Apostles and unconsciously he taught me to look for the contents of the verse before me. That night he had come to Peter's words on the times of refreshing that come from the presence of the Lord (Acts 3:19), and there, leaping out of the verse, was that one word 'refreshing'. So Dr Lloyd-Jones used it as God's highway into that verse. He said:

> What, then, is the gospel message? 'Repent ye therefore,' said Peter, 'and be converted, that your sins may be blotted out, when the times of refreshing shall come from the presence of the Lord.' This is Christianity. It is not a kind of conference to decide whether we have enough energy left to make a hole in the wall so that we can let in some air. No, no, it is not that. It is a message that comes from the outside — from the presence

of the Lord, the one Peter had been preaching about. It is the coming of the Son of God into this world that changes everything. This is the message of salvation. He can do it, and he alone can do it.

Do you know what civilization is? Have you ever been in the conditions that I am describing to you? Have you ever been in some of those cities in America where there is terrible humidity? In America they not only measure the heat, they measure the humidity, and they are quite right. Have you ever been in the city of Boston, say, on a hot August Sunday afternoon when it is not only very hot, but very humid as well? No sun to be seen, but it is there above the clouds.

The whole universe seems to be pressing down upon you, hot and humid. And you are tired, and you sit in a room and what can be done? Before they had air conditioning, people used to put on electric fans. The electric fan causes the air to circulate and while you are sitting somewhere near this fan you feel a little cooler. You are quite convinced that the fan is cooling the atmosphere. But you are wrong. It is actually increasing the temperature because the energy of the electricity is adding to the temperature. You have the impression that it is cooling the air, because there is a movement, but the fan does not bring in any fresh air at all. It makes the same air go round and round. You merely get the illusion that the position is being dealt with.

That is all civilization does. It does not touch the problem. It does not make any difference to the real condition of men and women. We change this and improve that, and there is a sort of movement, but nothing new is brought in. Let me use a medical illustration. You cure one disease and you say, 'Now we shall be all right.' Then you suddenly hear that another disease has come. Penicillin cures some of the most terrible diseases, yes, but that, in turn, produces certain germs that are resistant to penicillin and they are the real killers.[1]

Isn't that graphic? Here is mere 'man', Lloyd-Jones's constant theme, man in rebellion against God, doing everything to cool and perfume the stench of modern life without God, and all he does meets with little success. Then there is the refreshing that comes from God when Jesus Christ comes into a life, into a congregation, into a home, into a community.

Bad form can ruin good content. How do you make a sermon more interesting? You do the familiar basics like cultivating a conversational rather than a literary style. You explain any history, the people the Bible mentions, theological words, any cultural practices. You look at it from this angle and another, and make it all simply fascinating to the people. You tell the story that is in the biblical narrative, and you look for any vivid words as I have just described. You ask, what is the big story behind this little story? You try to flee from clichés and employ phrases that are memorable. One phrase that was given to me over twenty years ago was Harvey Cox's 'creative disaffiliation' and it provided a helpful angle on my relationship with our Anglican friends.

We also use illustrations. There is a fine chapter in Stuart Olyott's *Preaching, Pure and Simple*, entitled 'Vivid Illustration', which will help every minister.[2] Study it. I have a favourite memory that has done me much good and has brought to the affections of a congregation the demands of godly living. I was preaching in Louisville, Mississippi, and on the Monday morning when preaching was over I went to visit a friend of mine, a Baptist deacon whose daughter has married a PCA minister. He runs a furniture shop in the middle of town; I went to the store and talked with him there. There is not much going on in a little Mississippi town on a Monday morning and as we could relax and fellowship he told me how the previous week he had met this black Christian brother and they were talking together in the main street. Then up to them strutted a horrible white racist. He stopped and listened to their conversation for a while and then he turned to the black man and muttered something utterly unacceptable, words quite unspeakable such as I have never heard in all the time I have spent in Mississippi. My friend was shocked, and he turned to this blaggard and said heatedly,

'You shouldn't say a thing like that. You should be ashamed of yourself. You apologize to him for saying that.' This racist said, 'You won't find me apologizing to a black *epithet*', and off he strutted. My friend was so apologetic, he wanted to apologize for the whole white race and for this evil especially, the ugliness of what he had just seen and heard. 'I am so sorry', he said continually. 'It is alright', the black Christian said. 'It really is alright.' Then he added, 'You know, I would like to get my revenge on that man, and this would be my revenge. I would be driving back to Louisville late one night after eleven o'clock, and I would see his car at the side of the road. He had a flat tyre, and he did not have a jack, and I would stop my car and I would get out my jack and I would jack up his car and I would change his tyre for him. That would be the revenge I'd like to have on him.' It is a wonderful illustration of the New Testament ethic. Islamic suicide bomber, hear me! Don't overcome evil with evil, but overcome evil with good. If your enemy hungers, feed him, if he is thirsty, give him a drink; you pour coals of fire on his head.

I am not speaking of developing an obsessive mentality which is desperate for illustrations. Sermons do not consist of stringing together seven or so big illustrations, so that every few minutes you are launching forth onto another story. I do not think that is helpful preaching; in fact I think it is pathetic preaching. It is Jackanory rather than Whitefield. I do not believe that it is biblical preaching, but I do believe a judicious use of vivid words and illustrations is indispensable.

Another way to make preaching interesting is in good bodily actions. Here is an excursus; Dr Lloyd-Jones had a pose in singing hymns, head down, no bodily movement. He sang the words reverently with his eyes on the book. He hated every form of histrionic in hymn-singing. It was a surprise to worship at chapel services at Westminster Seminary with John Murray and see him singing with his hymn book held in outstretched arms which moved up and down and from side to side, so vigorously involved in the praise of God.

That was not the Doctor's style of singing; but when he preached, how he moved around that pulpit in Westminster

Chapel! He walked from side to side, speaking and gesturing, seeking to involve everyone in the congregation in the message of Jesus Christ, offering the Saviour and his salvation to them all. Someone said to me, 'He bounced around that pulpit!' That is not a metaphor one usually associates with Martyn Lloyd-Jones. Charles Haddon Spurgeon has a lecture on gestures during preaching, in his *Lectures to my Students*. The gestures are actually drawn there. If you have seen them, how delightful they are. That he should do that indicates that he did not believe bodily animation in the pulpit to be insignificant, or degrading to the ministry. Spurgeon had a fear of men failing to move a congregation because of gestures that were wooden or awkward or ill-timed — for example, unfortunate gestures that come from the elbow rather than the shoulder. I would not belittle the costly exercise of watching oneself preach on video and consequently seeking to iron out gauche and cumbersome gestures before they become a constant distraction. You know that gestures are contagious. I picked up a gesture from John Murray forty-three years ago. It is a sort of dive from the shoulder. I do it and I got it from him. He would lean into a certain pose to get a point across. I picked it up straightaway. People say that the students who have sat under my ministry have picked up my gestures. They know that I have had my influence on them, not by the purity of their lives (!), nor by the profundity of their theology (!), but for the way they wave about their arms which, alas, they have picked up from me.

Or again there is the preacher who smiles all the time; maybe it is his nerves, or maybe his mother told him when he began preaching that he should smile at the congregation. Whatever the reason, it wearies and turns people off. They refer to him as the Rev. Smiler — the rosy cheeks, the bushy white sideburns, the bald head and the smiling mouth out of which the ditties come: 'If I were a bumble bee...' God save his sheep from shepherds who encourage such sanctimonious twaddle. There is deep seriousness about our calling. We know the terrors of God and we are persuading men to hear and change. They are on a broad road that leads to destruction; we are sounding an alarm and there are words of grief for those who continually reject. Jesus wept.

Of course there are the opposite expressions. I think of the modernists I heard for the first fifteen years of my life. In my memory of them they seem such grey men, stern and moralistic. How can you preach the love of God or the good news of eternal life as God's gift if you are the Reverend Sourpuss? What tender woman would say yes to a marriage proposal from such a man? Let us avoid the stiff-as-a-board delivery; let us find grace to wipe away expressionless faces. Read the Scriptures. There is pathos, there is joy that is unspeakable and full of glory, and there is also groaning. Christ throws himself to the ground and his sorrow seems to be killing him. All are legitimate feelings for the preacher. I am saying to you by every legitimate means of true renewed humanity and grace and knowledge of the Bible make your sermons living and gripping. We are not interesting people in ourselves, and we are not members of interesting congregations. The only interesting thing about us is our message about the Lord Jesus Christ. That is the most fascinating news the world has ever heard or ever will.

Sermons that are well-structured

Fourthly a good Nonconformist sermon should be well-organized. There are points and they are as sturdy as steel and they undergird the whole. They are arranged in a logical order but the points do not protrude. In other words the Nonconformist preacher does not bore us with unnecessary 'firstlies', 'secondlies', 'thirdlies' and then sub-section minor 'firstlies' and 'secondlies' and 'thirdlies'. Such details are a distraction and confusing when they are meant to clarify. Is this 'thirdly' a main point or a sub-point to the 'secondly'? I do believe Dr Lloyd-Jones could have been more helpful in warning of steps forward in the progress and development of his sermons, by greater use of 'secondly' and 'thirdly'. Everyone's minds must wander during preaching. That is part of the sermon, to plant thoughts in people's brains. Drawing them in again to listen to

your preaching is difficult and one way is to say, 'Now thirdly...'
Then everyone freshens up again to journey on with you on a
new section. Please read, in Stuart Olyott's *Preaching Pure and
Simple*, his third chapter entitled 'Clear Structure'.

I will draw your minds in by announcing that this is the
beginning of a new paragraph. Our entire focus as we deal
with our text is set on the intent of the Holy Spirit in these
verses, what he has said, why he said it, and how he said it.
Asking those questions will immediately produce a structure of
answers. I would work on the set passage of Scripture for this
coming Lord's Day and arrange and rearrange truths until I
could see my outline. When I have my skeleton — with some
development, a good movement and a progression to a climax
— then the main battle for the sermon is over.

One thing more about the structure (and this I learned from
Jay Adams) is to understand the distinction between a lecture
outline and a preaching outline. This is simple and crucial. For
example, in a lecture you have written at the top of your page
(or certainly in your mind's eye) some such statement as this,
'The theme of this address is personal witnessing.' However, in
a true preaching outline there will be at the top of the outline,
not a thematic statement but a statement of purpose that will
read something like this, 'My purpose is to encourage you to
witness personally.' The lecture approach cues that speaker to
teach a topic as information, while the purpose statement pre-
pares the preacher to exhort people about their daily living.

But as Jay Adams says:

The contrast does not stop with the cuing statement at
the top of the outline. It extends to the entire outline.
Here are two examples:

Lecture Format
The Gifts of the Spirit
I. The source of the Corinthians' gift.
II. The functions of the Corinthians' gift.
III. The purpose of the Corinthians' gift.

Preaching Format
Use Your Spiritual Gifts
I. God gave each of you gifts.
II. God gave you them to use.
III. God gave them to use for the benefit of
     others.

Notice the differences, not only in the titles, but throughout. Of course, I have included only the major heads,
but the same thing holds true for subordinate points that
is true for these major heads. These titles differ: one is
abstract, the other personal; one is factual, the other is
motivational. The main points are different: those in one
are abstract, in the other personal; in one, the focus is
on the Corinthians, in the other on the congregation.
You can see clearly, can't you, that the preaching format continually cues the preacher to be personal, to
address his congregation, to bring them face to face
with God and his requirements; in short, it cues him to
preach. The lecture format cues the speaker to lecture
about, not to preach to.[3]

I think that this is important, and exhort you to take it to heart
and search your own style of preaching.

Sermons that are evangelistic

Fifthly, good Nonconformist preaching is evangelistic. I wonder,
has the evangelical church lost sight of the evangel? Watch the
tele-evangelists for a few minutes, call in on those channels to
judge for yourself. I rarely hear the gospel when I have let their
words enter my front room. I never hear sin being preached. I
rarely hear the comprehensive answer to man's need of Jesus
Christ, the Saviour as our prophet, priest and king. I rarely hear
him being offered and people being besought to believe and
trust in him. It seems to me that those men and women (and
there are as many women preaching on television as men)
have all lost the gospel.

There are others who are not on television who (a) preach just one narrow gospel strand of revealed religion — 'the Book, the Blood and the Blessed Hope' — and hardly anything else. There are yet others who (b) preach all the rest of the counsel of God in all the books of the Bible as if they were unrelated to the evangelistic imperative of the great commission.

The first group of preachers (a) have in some ways chosen the easiest way as far as preparation is concerned. Whatever the text, from whatever part of the Bible, they preach what they call 'the gospel' constantly, adding different illustrations to the message and ending with an invitation. Often such preaching shows hurriedness, lack of preparation and lack of thought about the objections to the Christian faith that people have today. Young people, boys on motorcycles and girls who work at McDonald's, quickly speak of why they can't believe in God, and their reason for not following the Lord Jesus Christ. The people sitting before us often hear those objections. Are we answering them in our evangelism? Are we evangelizing by overwhelming those objections with the superior and entirely satisfying truths of God? So there is the first group of preachers who have the narrowest understanding of evangelizing unbelievers. The problem we have with them is that their focus is on man's will. Their thinking is that they have to bring people to make a decision, but they need to step back and ask why their hearers are saying no to Jesus Christ. Do they see his beauty? Are they being given glimpses of it, in his person as God and man, in his offices as Prophet, Priest and King? Do they see why they need him because of their own sin and guilt? Before summoning them to a decision, preachers need first to display freshly the glories of Christ in his person and work as he is offered to us.

Read Dr Lloyd-Jones's evangelistic books, the sermons so owned of God to the conversion of many in Sandfields, or his preaching on the Acts of the Apostles. They provide for us his conception of what evangelism really is. It is quite awesome to see the respect he pays to the congregation's questions about the nature of Christianity, and his willingness to be involved at that level in their thinking. His hearers were meeting constant opposition to Christianity; in South Wales, the rise of socialism in the steel works of Aberavon and mines of the Afon valley was creating a generation who was dismissing the Bible. How demoralizing it might have been to men who were following the Saviour, but Lloyd-Jones showed the inadequacies of such thinking and the utterly sufficient answers in the truth that is in Jesus Christ. Evangelism is much more than preaching the blood of Jesus Christ each Sunday night to a congregation who can guess what the next sentence is going to be.

Then there is the second group of ministers (b) who major in expository preaching in a teaching ministry. It is helpful to teach sections of Scripture, but one drawback is what Americans call a cookie-cutter approach (and which we Welsh people call a Welsh-cake cutter approach) to a section of Scripture. Within passages of the Bible are 'gems of truth'. It is so unfashionable to say that today, but though all Scripture is equally God-breathed it is not all of equal significance. The six chapters that begin the first book of Chronicles are not as important as the six chapters of the letter to the Ephesians. There are also within smaller pericopes of revelation, truths that leap out at the reader. I fear that these Himalayas within divine revelation are being flattened into a plain as they are compassed within one section of Scripture being explained to a congregation.

In other words, in a certain section of Scripture there is a 'big verse', golden words full of ravishing meaning, a beautiful truth that people write out and pin on their notice-boards and stand on their desks. O let me taste this nectar and run for hours in its strength! But the preacher is so committed to going through, say, the book of Ephesians in twenty sermons, that he has no time to stop and consider these truths in their multi-faceted glory. He and his team of preachers, the co-pastor and assistant pastors, have divided up the series on this book of the Bible between them, and he can deal with this majestic diamond only *en passant*. It has been absorbed into the bigger passage and it is given the same sort of significance as the verses that precede it and the verses that follow it. I say that glorious mountains are being rolled out into a plain. Great right-angled truths that humble the proud are being blunted. This system is not serving the needs of dying sinners.

I am pleading for flexibility and the power to receive a gift God gives in such a truth as that. Congregations delight in hearing a man of God opening up one of these 'big verses'. I am pleading for you to pause; do slow down. Isn't preaching saying to a congregation, 'Look at this ... consider this glory...'? A craftsman will pick up an object he has created and will show you its particular beauty. A farmer will pull across with his crook a pedigree sheep that he is sending to an agricultural show. He will show you the distinctive features that make it a possible gold medal winner. An art teacher will point out the reasons why an Old Master is magnificent. When my friend Dick de Witt went to Colombia from Grand Rapids (he is a little older than I), he reckoned that this charge would probably be his last church. He told me he hoped to spend the rest of ministry preaching on the big verses of the Bible. I am talking about the verses Spurgeon preached on, or the truths Dr Lloyd-Jones toured with when during a year he would make his forty visits to mid-week congregations over the length and breadth of our land. He would preach his best sermons from his previous year of labours at Westminster Chapel. They were the greatest sermons any man could ever hear in the twentieth century. They were on such themes as Felix trembling as Paul reasoned with him of righteousness, temperance and judgement to come, or they were on a verse like this: 'How shall we escape if we neglect so great salvation?' Or he would open up the phrase, 'But God...' from Ephesians chapter two. I savour the memory of them still, though it is almost half a century since I first heard him.

Don't begin your ministry by doing what I did, preaching slowly through Genesis on Sunday mornings and Matthew at night. One of those series might have been fine, though I pause about commending a man fresh out of a seminary like London Theological Seminary or Westminster Theological Seminary to begin to pastor a church by bringing the congregation a student's mindset on Genesis. I did not have the equipment to preach those two series and it took a thick-skulled self-confident young man some years to realize that. How in the world did I survive? God was merciful. It would have been better in one series to have learned my craft and cut my teeth by preaching on the big truths of the Word of God. I am saying, do a Lloyd-Jones in the mornings and a Spurgeon in the evenings, certainly to start off.

So what else can you say about evangelism? Certainly the ideal is to include a statement of the gospel in every message. Even though half of our regularly preached messages might not be predominantly evangelistic in their focus certainly those messages too should contain saving knowledge for the stranger who has come in. Belief in Jesus Christ is essential to understanding or doing whatever the passage is requiring of you. You say to a congregation, 'How can you pray, or live like this unless you have been given a new heart, unless your trust is in Jesus Christ, and God has regenerated you? So then living as a husband should live, or obeying as a child is supposed to, you need to become a new creation of God to do this. In other words...' Thus the ethical becomes a door to the evangelistic. All the time you are conscious of man's need of grace, and you make the people conscious that they are in sin if they are not in Christ.

Again always you must discover the relevance of the death and the resurrection of Christ to whatever it is you are teaching. You see that, for example, where Paul is talking about tensions in the Philippian congregation. He is pleading that a certain mindset be in them; he talks of the incarnation of God the Son. He brings Christ into the problem of two women refusing to be of one mind. 'Have you ever considered the mind of the self-humbling God, the one who went even to the death of the cross?' he asks. Men and women should respect one another, be giving to one another and gracious to one another. When he talks about a husband loving his wife, Paul must take them to Golgotha. When the apostle talks about giving money to the cause of the kingdom, then he brings the cross in. 'Thanks be to God for his unspeakable gift!' The light of Jesus Christ falls across the whole Bible and he illuminates every aspect of the Christian life. You cannot preach on any passage from the Old or New Testament without in some way relating it to this heart of the gospel. Men of God preach the gospel from everywhere because it is everywhere. It does not stand alone; like yeast it permeates and lifts the whole. There is life that goes to every part of the Scripture. That will encourage the congregation themselves to become gospel preachers.

Sermons that are practical and applicatory

Sixthly, good Nonconformist preaching is practical and applicatory. That is, it is carefully adapted to the congregation to whom it is being preached. We persist in telling people not only what they should do as Christians but how to live according to God's will. An exclusive diet of 'how to' sermons is hardly inspirational but there are times, as with our Lord's Sermon on the Mount when he tells his hearers what is to be done or how not to do something — don't pray like this, don't fast in this way, don't give in this splashy manner. He tells them that the Pharisees behave like that, and they are hypocrites. Our Lord had spent thirty years thinking about what biblical principles meant and thus he applied them to the twelve, and also the other people who were following him.

Sermons must be applied. Think of the Lord Jesus Christ, how it was his custom every Sabbath to go the synagogue. A synagogue congregation in the first century was asked to consider a passage or theme and to look at it in the light of different rabbinic interpretations. Speaker and congregation were all looking at 'the thought for the day'. They were a crowd of onlookers. They were spectators. They were positioning themselves outside a certain theme, sometimes outside a certain passage. They were like a group of vacationers and the preacher was the tour guide. So he stops by a ruin where there is a plaque on the wall and they begin to look at it. He talks about it and they are all staring at it together. He tells them what the inscription says and that is it. He himself is not at all central to the event; the people don't see him. He is the cameraman who zooms in on something.

When Jesus went to the synagogue, he read the Scriptures, gave the scroll back to the attendant and sat down to preach.

Do you know the famous words that describe what happened
next? The eyes of everyone in the synagogue were fastened on
him. Then he began to confront them with the Word of God;
there were only two participants in the building, the preacher
and the assembly. They were not looking at and 'doing' a passage. He was confronting them with what God said to them
through his Word. He was a practical preacher. He was never
academic in his preaching. He was not interested in abstrac-
tions. He was dealing with the people that were before him. He
cared nothing for the unfolding of ideas even from the Bible
unless he could apply them to the conduct of his hearers. When
he spoke to people he did so within this kind of structure: 'but I
say to you ... Woe to you, scribes and Pharisees ... you should
not be surprised that I say to you, you must be born again ... I
tell you the truth, you are going to see the heavens opened and
the angels ascending and descending upon the Son of Man...'

There are hundreds of examples such as that, of Jesus
speaking directly to his hearers, 'I say to you...', by way of
warning, encouragement, promise or invitation. Jesus was not
first a Bible preacher or an expository preacher. He was God's
herald. He was bringing the Word of God to these people. He
certainly was not sharing things with them; he did not descend
to that. A sharer is not on the spot. A sharer does not have to
manifest a divine authority indicating that the Spirit of the Lord
is upon him; God anointed him not to share but to preach the
message of the gospel to men and women. How can you hold
someone accountable when he says, 'We only want to share
a few things with you?' We preachers are not called upon to
share the gospel but to declare the whole counsel of God and
beseech men and women to receive it. The idea of sharing suggests that the speaker is saying something incomplete; there is
just one angle on things which he has, while the joint corporate
experience of everyone else pitching in is going to complement
it. Such a man is just one person in the congregation and his
experience is part of the body life of the whole; sharing puts
him and the congregation alike upon the same footing. Yes,
let everyone minister to everyone else in corporate sanctification. What a powerful means of grace it is seven days a week

and twenty-four hours a day, for every believer to pray for one another and encourage one another. But there is more. The preacher is a called man, a divinely authorized servant of God. 'Woe is me if I do not preach the gospel', he says. His model is the Lord preaching the Sermon on the Mount and going through many of the Ten Commandments. He opened them out and he explained what doing God's will involves, and what the standards are. There was much misunderstanding in the land. The cultural consensus was confused, but Christ applied God's will to all who had ears to hear. He preached the inwardness of sin, subtlety of evil and divine obligation. He laid the Word of God on his hearers. They needed his light and leadership.

There is a kind of preaching that has become popular. Its emphasis is on the Bible's history of redemption and it claims to be the group that is really preaching Scripture. It is characterized by taking large sweeps across the biblical landscape; it can travel across centuries with ease and then it will give minute details about a word or phrase. People sit under such a ministry equipped with a pen and a notebook. The preacher will use an overhead projector and a PowerPoint presentation. He will slip onto the screen his outline, neatly written, sub-point by sub-point. What is my point? The whole emphasis is on knowledge. The whole thrust is to inform the mind. It is too much of a cerebral event. There is no confrontation. PowerPoint dulls everything. There is little application. There is no focus on the affections of men and women. In other words, it is done so that the hearers will understand a passage of the Bible better. It is not done so that they will love the God of the Bible with all their heart, soul, mind and strength. A man proposing marriage to the girl of his dreams would disdain PowerPoint in how he tells her of his love. The thinking behind this widespread movement is not of a congregation broken over their sins fleeing to Jesus Christ for salvation. The focus is on the intellect and a certain passage of the Bible, but even demons have a great grasp of the exegesis of Scripture. Milton, in one place in *Paradise Lost*, portrays them gathered in the caverns of hell discussing the divine determinism, and doing so with great accuracy I suppose.

Sermons that reflect a growing knowledge of God

Seventhly, everything the man of God is, he is before God. There is a renowned quotation of Dr Lloyd-Jones in his *Preaching and Preachers* in which he says:

> I can forgive a man for a bad sermon, I can forgive the preacher almost anything if he gives me a sense of God, if he gives me something for my soul, if he gives me the sense that, though he is inadequate himself, he is handling something which is very great and very glorious, if he gives me some dim glimpse of the majesty and the glory of God, the love of Christ my Saviour, and the magnificence of the Gospel. If he does that I am his debtor, and I am profoundly grateful to him.[4]

How can a man give to others a glimpse of the majesty and glory of God if he has not seen it himself? Sustained effectiveness in the ministry can only come in direct proportion to one's own spiritual vigour. Al Martin has set out this aphorism, that the man of God has to strive to maintain a real, expanding, varied and original acquaintance with God and his ways. How does this American preacher set that out? In what is one of the best quotations in a book about his theology of preaching he says the following:

> If the man of God is to have sustained effectiveness in his ministry, he must strive to maintain an acquaintance with God and His ways. This acquaintance must be *real*, as opposed to feigned, formal or professional. He must be apostolic in the sense that he can say, 'What we have seen and heard we proclaim to you also, so that you too may have fellowship with us; and indeed our fellowship is with the Father, and with His Son Jesus

Christ' (1 John 1:3). He must be a man who knows God other than by hearsay.

Furthermore, his acquaintance with God and His ways must be *expanding*. He is called to be transformed 'from one level of glory to another' (2 Cor. 3:18), he is called to 'grow in the grace and knowledge of our Lord and Savior Jesus Christ' (2 Pet. 3:18). This progressive transformation and growth is locked into the fact that God and His holy Word are both inexhaustible. If the man of God is not expanding in his acquaintance of God and His ways, he is failing as a Christian and his effectiveness as a pastor will be neutralized.

This acquaintance must not only be real and expanding, it must be *varied*. The ups and downs, the joys and sorrows, must be experienced. The Psalms, which cover the entirety of human emotion and experience, serve as a good guide. If the man of God is to know God, he must know Him in the darkness of night and the brightness of day, in the fullness of His presence (Ps. 16:11) and in the absence of His presence (Ps. 77:7-10).

This varied experience of God and His ways is obviously a first-hand experience. The acquaintance must be a *personal and individual* acquaintance. In this day of crass individualism, there is the danger of overemphasizing the personal and individual at the expense of solidarity and the corporate. Nevertheless, the Bible in its broad context of solidarity (in Adam, in Christ, in the faith, etc.) also presents a noble individualism where the hairs of a man's head are numbered (Matt. 10:30) and each one is called by name (John 10:3). So the man of God not only walks with his God corporately, but also individually'.[5]

Sermons that are effectual

Eighthly, good Nonconformist preaching is gripping. It is compelling and there is persuasiveness. We are told that the common people heard Jesus gladly. The teaching was often profound and even his disciples who heard some of those messages many times did not understand the parables. Messages were constantly provocative and controversial but there was something in them that gripped the hearers. They walked right around a lake to hear another sermon from him when he had sailed across to the other side, or men followed him in their thousands to listen to his preaching, hanging on to every word.

I remember in September 1958, I had heard in camps, particularly from the Presbyterian students who were the officers, respectful and affectionate references to 'the Doctor'. Who was this man they called 'the Doctor'? Then a month before I began university, while still a teenager, I saw in the *Western Mail* that 'the Doctor' was coming to preach at the ordination service of Dr Eifion Evans at the Memorial Hall in Cardiff. I took a train from Barry, walked along Cowbridge Road from Cardiff General Station and sat in that packed Forward Movement Hall looking around at the congregation. It was a black suited congregation, a hatted congregation, a serious-minded congregation, and such a singing congregation when they sang 'A debtor to mercy alone'.

There he was in the flesh and I told him twenty years later that this was the first time I had heard him. 'I don't remember what you preached on', I said. He did not appear to like that, but it was true. I just knew that this was a very important occasion and I needed to understand why. It took just that one message to adjust to that level of piety, reasoning, encounter, seriousness and truth that I had been deprived of for so long. He told me, 'You know what I preached on', and he told me the passage. But I could not remember. He added, 'You know how I said that Eifion Evans was going to be a pharmacist, and suddenly God touched him and changed the whole direction of his life. He became an ambassador for God.' 'I can't remember', I said. He told me of someone who had had such a blessing in that meeting. I too had had a blessing and I was sorry I could not remember the words of Lloyd-Jones, just the Word, great, golden, full of God and utterly magnificent. How fascinating it all was. The gospel came not in word only but in power and in the Holy Spirit and with much assurance.

Should one not expect some such phenomenon, as God lives, and we are his appointed servants? Should it not be like that? Should the absence of those confirming signs of the work of God not deeply grieve us today? I am referring to their absence from the pulpit in which I have stood and preached for forty years, of the gospel coming in a gripping way so that men know that it is with the Holy Spirit sent down from heaven.

Consider the preaching of the Lord Jesus and the great impact he made. In John chapter seven, we have the incident of the Pharisees sending their bully boys to arrest Christ. Off they go, these yokels, and Jesus is in the temple saying things like, 'If any man thirst, let him come unto me and drink; out of his belly will flow rivers of living water, and he said that of the Spirit that was to be given to those who believed in him.' Those two men tried to get through to him but the crowds were packed like sardines, and as far as his voice carried they stood, sitting on window sills, standing around the doors and on the walls. No one was prepared to give way lest they should fail to hear one Word of life. So those country boys grated to a halt in the crowd and they had to stand and listen with everyone else. They too came under the power of the Word; those who had come to arrest remained to pray. Finally when Jesus ended his sermon, and the crowd slowly and quietly moved away, those young men knew that they had to return to give account to their employers the Pharisees. They knocked the door and went in; the Pharisees asked where Jesus was. 'We sent you to get him. Why are you here empty-handed?' The spokesman said, 'Never man spake like this man. We never heard anyone speak like that in our lives before.' The words of Jesus had turned wolves into puppy dogs. No miracles were done that day; just the Word of the Lord spoken with divine energy, and thus it has been throughout history. When they heard that reply the Pharisees were so afraid. If men who had been in their pockets and pay could be captivated by Jesus then who could be safe?

I learn one lesson from this, that the great antidote to doubt is to sit under the best ministry you can. Another lesson is to do

what Al Martin exhorts: never stop developing a real, expanding, varied and original acquaintance with God and his ways.
My heroes have been men who are always thinking about new
portions of Scripture and new books to read and study, who
share with congregations the freshness and the delight of the
message of the gospel, and want in every way to declare that
Word of God.

> Happy if in my latest breath
> I might but gasp his name,
> Preach him to all and cry in death
> Behold, behold the lamb.
>
> *Charles Wesley*

I want to live like that and I want to die like that too.

Sermons that are relevant to every hearer

Ninthly, good Nonconformist preaching is confident about the
relevance of what it has to say to every single person. The Lord
Jesus ended the Sermon on the Mount by telling his hearers
about two builders. I once was listening to Dr Lloyd-Jones in
Aberystwyth when at the close of the sermon he described
these two men. He had just told the story that we know so well
of the one rapidly building his house, planting his garden and
sitting on his porch looking scornfully at the other man who
was still laying the foundation. Then the storm comes...

Let me digress ... I had taken my nine-year-old daughter
to that service and as we walked home together afterwards I
asked her, 'What did you think of that?' She replied, 'It was like
Sunday mornings ... only simpler.' I made sure Dr. Lloyd-Jones
heard that. I thought that would encourage him. If you can
capture children, and speak so that young people take heed,
then is the future of the church secure. The Doctor's preaching
had captured my little girl.

...So the storm came and hit both these houses and one
collapsed like a house of cards while the other withstood everything which the elements hurled at it. What is the purpose of

that parable? The man whose life is built on Jesus Christ – a little girl whose life is built on Jesus Christ – is absolutely safe. Even the gates of hell will not destroy her, because she is building her life on the Lord Jesus Christ, upon his teaching, and while she does that her life is inviolable.

Our Lord was looking ahead to the twenty-first century, the utterly secularized Europe in which you and I live, the carnality and materialism, the anti-Christian spirit, the wickedness that is all around us today, and the pressures on ordinary people who love and serve the Lord Jesus Christ to renege. The Son of God says, 'It is alright. I will keep every one of them as they build their lives on me; they are safe. I won't lose any one of those that the Father has given to me. They will be secure from all attacks and alarms.' Our Lord Jesus Christ was confident that his message, his very words, were relevant for every single person who comes to church. To every person we talk to, we have something of the deepest importance for their personal lives. We can say to every single person in this great city of London — and you know that a great city is a great sin — 'I have good news for you. I have a Saviour that I can offer to you. A prophet who will teach you what is true, a priest who lays down his life for sinners like you and lives in heaven to intercede for them, a king who will keep you all your life on a narrow path, but that way leads to eternal life. I am offering him to you. That is my good news for you.' We have a message that we can tell to all men and women — the extraordinary relevance of the gospel of Jesus Christ to all men and women. Compared to Christ nothing else matters.

In what has been an awful twentieth century for my own Principality, where philosophical speculation, modernism, socialism, capitalism, nationalism and all the isms of the world have sought to put the gospel of Jesus Christ into second place, we have seen that Bible preachers are still there. But what pain we find everywhere. The first chapter of Romans is not just a description of evil, but it is also the description of anguish. That is the civilization in which we live. But this Saviour has something to say to every person who lives in this age. Our Lord is confident of his relevance to every single person and that is the confidence that underlies all real Nonconformist preaching.

I have finished, but I can't give a nine point lecture. There must be ten, must there not? The number insists that it be so! Then let me add this from Dr Lloyd-Jones: he must have the last word.

Sermons that change people

Tenthly, Nonconformist preaching does something for the souls of men.

> Any true definition of preaching must say that that man is there to deliver the message of God ... He has been sent, he is a commissioned person, and he is standing there as the mouthpiece of God and of Christ to address these people ... He is there to influence people ... Preaching should make such a difference to a man who is listening that he is never the same again. Preaching, in other words, is a transaction between the preacher and the listener. It does something for the soul of man, for the whole of the person, the entire man; it deals with him in a vital and radical manner.[6]

May such preaching be heard again in every town in our nation!

Chapter 5

The Carr's Lane Succession: The Decline of Nonconformity as Seen in the Light of the Ministries of John Angel James, R. W. Dale and J. H. Jowett

Kenneth Brownell

As an undergraduate, I studied modern British history. One of the books that I was assigned to read was George Dangerfield's *The Strange Death of Liberal England*. This is a brilliant account of how the great Liberal Party of the late nineteenth century disintegrated and almost vanished in the early twentieth century. I think that a similar book could be written and entitled *The Strange Death of Nonconformist England*. Political Liberalism and religious Nonconformity were closely linked in the late nineteenth century and the decline of both movements is one of the most striking in the twentieth century. This is what struck the historian D. W. Brogan in 1943. He wrote:

> It is probable that Nonconformity reached its height of political power, was most representative of the temper of the English people, round the beginning of this century ... But in the generation that has passed since the great Liberal landslide of 1906, one of the greatest changes in the English religious and social landscape has been the decline of Nonconformity.[1]

Strangely, Dangerfield barely mentions Nonconformity, which in itself is indicative of how much it had disappeared from the social and political landscape by the time he wrote the book in 1970.

The purpose of this paper is to attempt to account for the remarkable decline of Nonconformity. Nonconformity was a very complex phenomenon and a full explanation of its decline would have to take account of a number of social, political and cultural factors as well as theological and spiritual ones. For our purposes, I will focus on the theological and spiritual factors. Our concern here is not so much with the political, social and cultural significance of Nonconformity as with its theological and spiritual significance. The latter has some bearing on the former, but that is not our primary concern. Rather we want to explore why Nonconformity declined as a spiritual force in British society and draw some lessons for ourselves from what we discover. In doing this we need to bear in mind the context of the general decline of institutional Christianity in Britain. In recent years, there has been much discussion about the secularization of British society. Some date the beginning of secularization in the nineteenth century, whereas others, such as Calum Brown, date it from the 1960s. Whatever the case, Nonconformity was caught up in the process and it is an illusion to think that, had the churches only remained theologically orthodox or undertaken certain strategies, things would have been significantly different. I am not even sure that, in the changed social and cultural climate, a revival would have made much difference. Nevertheless there were certain spiritual and theological factors that contributed to the decline and these we want to explore.

I want to do this in the light of the successive ministries of John Angel James, R. W. Dale and J. H. Jowett at Carr's Lane Meeting House in Birmingham. The ministries of these three remarkable men covered the period from 1804, when James became minister, to 1911, when Jowett resigned after being called to become minister of Fifth Avenue Presbyterian church in New York City. These ministries covered the period of Nonconformity's great expansion to the beginning of its decline.

There are several reasons for focusing on one church and its succession of ministers. I believe that it will enable us to gain some depth in what is a very big subject. While not every aspect of Nonconformity's decline can be covered, this approach will help us see what happened in one of its flagship congregations. Moreover because these three men were important leaders of Nonconformity in general, and Congregationalism in particular, we will be able to see at close hand how they rose to the challenges of their times. However, it may seem strange to some to look for answers for Nonconformity's decline in what was one of its most successful churches, at a time when Nonconformity was at its strongest. I think it good to do so, for the same reason that if you want an explanation for the decline of, say, the British Empire, it is best to look at it in its prime, where you can see the weaknesses that would lead to its decline.

Before we look at the Carr's Lane succession, let me paint a picture of Nonconformity at its height. In terms of numbers, it is thought that, by the end of the nineteenth century, about half the church-going population in England and Wales attended a Protestant Nonconformist chapel. The 1851 Religious Census, although much debated by historians and sociologists, revealed that just over forty per cent of the population attended a church service on 31 March of that year, and that just under half of those were Nonconformists, that is, 3,338,885 people or 18.62 per cent of the population. There were of course regional variations. In Wales, about 45.5 per cent of the population attended a chapel. There were similar but smaller variations in England, such as in Cornwall where Methodism was strong, or even in some of the old Dissenting heartlands. As we are looking at a Congregational church, it is worth noting the strength of Congregationalism. About 499,604 people, or 2.95 per cent of the population, attended a Congregational service. Our Victorian fathers were rather shocked at what they considered the low level of attendance, but historians and sociologists think that the census was taken at the peak of church attendance. Whatever they thought at the time, for Nonconformists the census represented a considerable growth since the eighteenth century. The 203 Congregational meeting-houses in 1715 had become 2,604 chapels by 1851, a growth rate of 751 per cent. The growth of Congregationalists, along with Baptists and Methodists, was due to the Great Awakening. In fact, the period of greatest expansion came between 1790 and 1830, as churches of all orthodox denominations aggressively evangelized the nation, reaping through their preaching, as Michael Watts has pointed out, seed that Anglicans had sown through their catechizing.[2] Although growth had slowed down by the second half of the nineteenth century, Nonconformist churches continued to grow. By 1900 there were 3,433 Congregational churches in England and Wales and, according to the *Daily News* survey of London churches in 1902-1903, of the one-fifth of Londoners who attended church, one-tenth attended one of 345 Congregational churches in the metropolitan area. It is thought that Congregationalism reached its peak around 1914.

However statistics do not tell the whole story. They do not tell us about the genuine spiritual life of Nonconformity, nor do they tell us about the world of Nonconformity at its peak. In our much-reduced circumstances, it is difficult to imagine the self-confidence, energy and sheer brio of Nonconformity at its peak. Perhaps we have to visit an American mega-church to find anything comparable. This was a world that was effectively an alternative religious culture to that of the Establishment. There were the popular preachers, such as C. H. Spurgeon, Joseph Parker, R. F. Horton, Alexander Maclaren, and R. W. Dale and J. H. Jowett whom we will consider. Parker drew large congregations to the City Temple in London with his dramatic preaching that often drew applause from the people and occasionally the pumping of umbrellas. A fervent evangelical, he was also a fervent Liberal, and he was not careful to keep the two distinct in his preaching. Also popular, but with a more middle class congregation, was R. F. Horton at Lyndhurst Road in Hampstead. One listener remembered a service in which: 'He leans forward with outstretched hands ... He is torn with bitter agony. His voice is shaken by the tumult of his feelings ... Outside someone touches you ... with a light greeting. It is like the breaking of a spell.' A woman remembered 'the silence of a great congregation, held by the power of an eloquence which we felt rather than understood, endued him with an "other-worldliness" which could not be explained'[3]. Something of that inexplicable magic may partly explain why Nonconformity declined, but at its best it also explains something of the power of Nonconformity. There is a story of the vicar of the parish church opposite Lyndhurst Road who ruefully pointed out to a visiting bishop the vast crowds entering the chapel. The bishop told him that if he preached the gospel like Dr Horton he might have the crowds as well. Incidentally, the Congregational church is today a block of flats, while the parish church is still operating.

But important as they were, Nonconformity was more than its preachers. There were congregations made up of people from mostly the middle and respectable lower ranks of society and a surprising number of younger men. There were chapels where congregations large and small met and where numerous societies and auxiliaries for every conceivable purpose had their homes. There were extensive social ministries that sought to relieve some of the problems of a growing industrial and urbanizing nation. There were great voluntary societies with their annual meetings. There were church and Sunday school anniversaries and ordination services. There were civically-minded Nonconformist citizens, some of them famous like Samuel Morley or Titus Salt, but most of them not, who did so much to transform the cities and towns of Britain. There were Nonconformist politicians with their famous conscience, who represented an important constituency of the Liberal Party of Gladstone, Rosebery, Campbell-Bannerman, Asquith and Lloyd-George, the last two brought up in Nonconformist homes. Like Victorian architecture, Victorian Nonconformity has been mocked and despised, but perhaps has more to be said for it than hitherto thought. But by the early twentieth century, all this was in decline. What happened? To find some answers let us turn and consider the Carr's Lane succession.

The Congregational church meeting in Carr's Lane Chapel was originally a secession from the Old Meeting in Birmingham by a Trinitarian minority. The chapel to which John Angel James came as minister in 1804 had been built in 1747 and was located in the centre of Birmingham. In the course of the three ministries, the area around the chapel would change significantly. At several points, the congregation considered moving to the suburbs, but did not, and sought to adapt to its changing circumstances. Because of its location and history the congregation always contained some influential citizens of Birmingham.

* * *

John Angel James was born and raised in Blandford Forum in Dorsetshire and brought up in a godly family of modest means. At a relatively young age he was apprenticed to a High Calvinist shoemaker in Poole. With some of the other apprentices he attended Bible studies and various local churches. At one point he almost became a Baptist but did not, something for which he later thanked God. Sensing a call to the ministry, James enrolled in David Bogue's academy in Gosport. In later years, James felt that, admirable as Bogue was as a preacher and promoter of missions, his education in his academy was far from adequate. In 1803, he visited Carr's Lane and made a great impression on the congregation. He felt at the time that he was preaching to an assembly of the ancients, but warmed to them and they to him, and he was called as minister the following year. The congregation was in a weakened state and remained so for several years. James felt very discouraged and was tempted to resign. But after seven years, things began to improve. The deacons made alterations to the building and the congregation began to increase in numbers. James was increasingly in demand as a preacher in churches and societies, such as the Bible Society and the London Missionary Society. A sermon before a meeting of the latter in London in 1812 was particularly notable. His theme was the centrality of the cross for missions. It was a long sermon and halfway through it he took a break; the congregation sang a hymn and threw oranges onto the platform for his refreshment. A new chapel was built in 1820 and James continued to minister there until his death in 1859.

During his ministry at Carr's Lane, James was not a stranger to controversy. He held strong views as a Dissenter and was highly critical of the Church of England. The early years of his ministry were a period of increasing tension between Church and Dissent. James was also a strong Congregationalist. He wrote on Congregational principles and was also active in denominational affairs, participating in the formation of the Congregational Union in 1831. A particular concern was ministerial training. James took a great interest in Spring Hill College in Birmingham and served on its board and as its chairman. But James was also a catholic-minded evangelical. He helped to form the Evangelical Alliance in 1841. Theologically, he was a warm-hearted Calvinist evangelical as shaped by the Great Awakening and its aftermath. His writings reflected this. Perhaps his best known work was *The Anxious Inquirer,* which was widely used by many inquiring about becoming Christians — not least by the young R. W. Dale.

How can James help us understand the decline of Dissent? It seems to me in two areas. James was always concerned about spiritual life. Towards the end of his life, he perceived a decline in spiritual life among ministers and members and a growing worldliness. In 1847, he gave an address at Cheshunt College in Hertfordshire that was later expanded and published as *An Earnest Ministry.* His basic thesis was stated in these terms: 'We live in an earnest age, and nothing but an earnest ministry can succeed in it.'[4] Earnestness he defined as a single-minded devotion to one supreme task. For the Nonconformist minister, that was the conversion of people to Christ. It was this earnestness that James saw was increasingly lacking in ministers, as well as an increase of worldliness. One of James's concerns in this regard was the piety of students in the various Congregational theological colleges. As I have mentioned, James was closely involved with Spring Hill College in Birmingham and was a strong advocate of a well-trained ministry. But throughout his life, he urged colleges to care for, and students to nurture, spiritual life. He was not alone in this. In 1844, a conference was held in Leicester in order to consult on the matter of theological education in the denomination. Along with other speakers, James emphasized the need of a godly as well as an educated ministry.[5]

Just over a decade later, James wrote a series of articles for the *Evangelical Magazine* entitled, 'What is the spiritual state of our churches?' R. Tudur Jones says that these articles were effectively his last will and testament to the churches. He saw among Christians an increasing worldliness in personal, family and church life. Again, he was concerned for the ministry which he saw as increasingly self-indulgent and effeminate. It was coming to value gifts and skills above godly character. Ours, he said, 'is an age of man-worship, the idolatry of genius'. Such was the seriousness of the situation that James feared for the future of evangelical Christianity.[6] James was not alone in detecting something wrong in the spiritual life of the churches. In 1849, Edward Miall had criticized the increasing respectability and complacency of Nonconformity in his *The British Churches in their relation to the British people.*

It seems to me that James and others put their fingers on a key reason for the decline of Nonconformity. Of course, it does not explain everything, but it must be taken into account. At the root of the decline of any movement is a waning of spiritual life. This is something that evangelicals today need to remember when assessing the contemporary condition of the church. The problem of the churches is fundamentally spiritual in nature. Of course, a revival of spiritual life will not solve all our problems or restore us to the heights from which we have fallen. But our concern is not for evangelical churches to be restored to a commanding position in society, but for them to be restored to the truth and to vital godliness. That was James's concern and that must be ours as well.

The other area that concerned James was a decline in theological orthodoxy. Until the end of James's ministry, Congregationalism had been almost entirely orthodox and Calvinistic in its theology, but during the 1850s that began to change. Two issues emerged at this time. The first was the question of eternal punishment. In 1846, Edward White published his *Life of Christ* in which he stated that since immortality was only in Christ, those who were not in Christ would be destroyed. In 1855, a controversy on the same issue broke out with the publication of a collection of hymns titled *The Rivulet* by the Congregationalist minister Thomas Toke Lynch. The other issue was the inspiration of the Bible. This came to the fore in the case relating to Samuel Davidson, a tutor at Lancashire Independent College.

In 1856, some pastors raised concerns with the college board about Davidson's teaching, particularly as it related to the Mosaic authorship of the Pentateuch. James was not directly involved in the controversy, but he was in correspondence with a number of eminent ministers who were. He was in no doubt that the board should dismiss Davidson for his teaching.

'If I were on the committee,' he wrote,

> I would sooner surrender the dearest friend I had on earth — if he were in such a situation, with such sentiments — than consent to keep him … I have heard that the students are on his side, and threaten to leave if he retires, or be dismissed. If I were on the committee I would consent to the clearance of the house, rather than swerve from what I deem to be a regard for the truth.[7]

Along with others, such as Spurgeon, James was apprehensive about the theological drift of Nonconformity. This concern is highlighted in a funeral sermon in 1852 for a colleague whose doctrine, James pointed out, was as sound at the end as it was at the beginning. He wondered whether 'the men of modern ideas' saw the number of conversions as the result of their preaching as did his departed friend. He went on: 'Let us have as much improvement as possible in logic, criticism, exegesis, rhetoric, philosophy, and elocution — the more the better, but God in his mercy save us from the impiety and folly of seeking after another Gospel'.[8] James's concerns proved well-founded, but sadly the door would be opened, even inadvertently, by his successors at Carr's Lane.

* * *

Five years before James's death, R. W. Dale became his assistant pastor at Carr's Lane. Dale was born in London in 1829. He was brought up by godly parents who attended the robustly Calvinistic ministry of the Scot, John Campbell, at Whitefield's Tabernacle on Tottenham Court Road. As a boy, he came under strong religious impressions and only came to faith after a long and agonizing struggle. Interestingly, one of the means by which he came to faith was James's book *An Anxious Inquirer*. Later, Dale would be mildly critical of the book for reasons we will see, but at the time he found it helpful, even if it may have prolonged his agony of soul. Feeling called to the ministry, Dale went to study at Spring Hill where he met James. James was very fond of this bright and spiritually-minded young man and did much to encourage him. In 1853, Dale gained a London M. A. with two prizes for knowledge of Hebrew and Greek. That year, the church at Carr's Lane called him as assistant pastor and the next year he became co-pastor. He succeeded James as pastor in 1859 and remained as such until his death in 1895. During his years at Carr's Lane, he preached faithfully to a large and influential congregation. He always worried that his preaching was too intellectual and lacked the common touch, but his congregation was devoted to him and it contained people of all classes. There was a passionate intensity in his preaching wedded to a rigorously logical mind. While his preaching was very doctrinal and expository it also had a strong moral and ethical tone to it.

The mystical element that one can detect in Spurgeon's preaching was lacking in Dale's. He was much more matter-of-fact and concerned for its immediate relevance to his hearers and the wider community. It was the community that will always be associated with Dale. Dale and late nineteenth-century Birmingham were almost synonymous. Once in Parliament, Joseph Chamberlain was chided for being the Member for Dr

Dale. Chamberlain replied that he was honoured to represent such a constituency. Dale saw it as part of his mission to be involved as a citizen of Birmingham and as such he sat on numerous committees and was consulted by civic leaders. But Dale was also committed to his denomination. He served as Chairman of the Congregational Union and helped to establish the International Congregational Council. At one point, Dale withdrew from involvement with the Union over a political difference, but there was never any doubting his commitment to Congregationalism. In fact, he wrote a classic guide to membership in Congregational churches and his last book, published posthumously, was a history of Congregationalism. He wrote many books and was in constant demand as a preacher around the country.

I want to explore three areas of Dale's thinking that shed some light on the decline of Nonconformity.

1. Dale's commitment to theological reconstruction

In his *An Earnest Ministry*, James rejected the idea that the historic doctrines of the faith had to be restated to meet the challenges of modern thought. He called it 'delusive and fatal'. 'What', he asked, 'are the discoveries of Newton, or of Davy; or the inventions of Watt, or of Arkwright, compared to these themes? Viewing man in relation to immortality, as sinful and accountable, what is art or science, compared with revealed truth?'[9] Dale did not agree with his mentor. Dale felt passionately that theological reconstruction was the greatest need of the hour. In an article in the *British Quarterly Review* he wrote:

> The theology of the Reformers and their immediate successors is beginning to show the operation of the silent forces of decay. In many parts of Protestant Europe it is sinking into ruins; and everywhere the work of reconstruction is necessary, if the Protestantism of the next century is to have a theology at all. Reconstruction, we say, is necessary — not repair. The philosophical methods of the present century are new; its exegesis is new;

and, although we believe that none of the great articles
of the Evangelical creed will be finally rejected, theological systems must be rebuilt from their foundations.[10]

Dale was deeply conversant with the cultural and philosophical, as well as the theological, trends of his times and felt deeply
their challenge to the Christian faith.

I think he was too impressed with them and, like many,
panicked. Compared to others, he was relatively conservative
in his reconstruction of theology, but in the end he was too in
awe of it to do what really needed to be done. In this, I think,
Dale is a warning to us. We need to engage with contemporary culture and theology, but if we are over-impressed by it
we are likely to concede too much. In some ways we have the
advantage of living on the other side of the liberal experiment
in reconstruction and can be more careful.

1. His rejection of Calvinism

Until well into the nineteenth century, most Congregationalists
were, like James, Calvinistic in their theology. Like many others of his generation Dale shed his Calvinism at an early stage.
Writing in 1877 he said, 'Among the present aspects of our
theological thought, perhaps none is most obvious than the
general disappearance of Calvinism'.[11] Dale shed his Calvinism
during his co-pastorate with James. Later in life he wrote: 'I
finally broke away from Calvinism very soon after I entered the
ministry'.

> When preaching through Romans he shocked the Carr's
> Lane congregation by rejecting the traditional doctrine
> of original sin and the imputation of Adam's guilt. As
> his son records, 'As the exposition advanced, excite-
> ment rapidly grew. Excitement deepened into alarm,
> and alarm rose to the height of panic. The discourses
> on the latter half of the fifth chapter marked the turning
> point. The congregation was like one great Bible class;
> there was an open Bible in almost every hand. Wave

upon wave of emotion rolled through the congregation
as the preacher developed his theme.[12]

On his part, James sought to calm the high feelings of people
and assure them that everything was all right. Dale himself was
very upset at the uproar and a short time later offered to resign,
but James persuaded him not to. Perhaps James's optimism
was the weakness of the Calvinists of his generation. Dale recorded a conversation with him:

> He once said to me with great energy — raising his arm
> and clenching his hand as he said it — 'I hold these
> doctrines of Calvinism with a firm grasp'. 'But', I said,
> 'you never preach about them'. 'Well', he replied, 'you
> know there is not much in the Bible about them'.[13]

But before long Dale had rejected Calvinism as a system, although he had a high regard for its intellectual rigour and the
spiritual and moral effect it had on its adherents at its best.
However he personally found it morally repugnant. 'I know
not how to repress my indignation; there are no words strong
enough to express my abhorrence, loathing and disgust'.[14]

Part of Dale's problem was, I think, that he was rejecting
the philosophical Calvinism or 'modern Calvinism' that had
been taught by theologians like Edward Williams, who had
earlier in the century sought to modify the high Calvinism
of some eighteenth-century Calvinists. Dale considered such
attempts to be 'Calvinism in decay'. Yet as much as he disliked
Calvinism, Dale lamented that there was no theology large and
grand enough to replace it. In an ordination sermon in 1890 he
bemoaned the doctrinal minimalism that characterized modern
Congregationalists. Their doctrinal statements were a poor
thing compared to the Savoy Declaration. 'The elaborate and
stately system of theological belief which had been created by
the theologians of the Reformed Church ... has been in decay
for two centuries. And, as of yet, no other organised theological
system has taken its place'.[15]

2. His acceptance of a fallible Bible

Like many in his generation Dale, accepted the idea of a fallible Bible. He felt the force of higher critical study of the Bible. In his 1869 address as the chairman of the Congregational Union, he said that the authority of Christ was not undermined in the current controversy by the 'demonstration of the historical untrustworthiness of a few chapters here and there in the Old Testament'. But he did feel keenly just how unsettling all this was for people in the churches. His integrity compelled him to face the issue, but he had to admit it created a measure of 'indecision and uncertainty'.[16]

In an ordination sermon in 1890, he urged the new pastor to take up critical issues if necessary, but to concentrate on the greater themes of the gospel. One of the things Dale sought to do in his preaching was to put the relationship of Christians to the living Christ beyond the reach of results of biblical criticism. In his 1890 book, *The Living Christ and the Four Gospels,* he argued that we can still have a relationship with Christ with a fallible Bible.[17] In fact, a fallible Bible removed any authority coming between the believer and Christ. The authority and reality of the living Christ was a great theme for Dale. His own experience on an Easter Sunday morning in the 1860s transformed his life and ministry and he longed for others to share this. It is interesting that Dale's view on Scripture did not seem to affect his preaching and how he handled the Bible. He was in fact relatively conservative on critical issues.

The trouble would come with later generations, when the fallible Bible would lose its credibility.

3. His annihilationism

I have mentioned already that in 1846 Edward White published his *Life of Christ,* in which he stated that, since immortality was only in Christ, then those who were not in Christ would be destroyed rather than suffer eternal punishment. Thomas Binney, the minister of the fashionable King's Weigh House Chapel in London, had taught this view for years. Later in 1855, the issue exploded into a controversy with the publication of a collection of hymns by Thomas Toke Lynch entitled *The Rivulet*.

While the controversy eventually calmed down, it was evident that in this area many Congregationalists were moving away from the traditional view. When White's book was republished in 1875, Dale among others supported him. The year before, he had publicly stated his annihilationist position in a paper before the Congregational Union.

> We have reached the conclusion that eternal life is the gift of the Lord Jesus Christ, that this life is not given to those who reject the gospel, but is given in the new birth to those who believe and who are thereby made partakers of the divine nature.[18]

He objected to the suggestion that his view undermined evangelism and missions.

In an address to the London Missionary Society, he argued that the gospel compelled Christians to preach to everyone everywhere.[19] Interestingly, his great admirer Robertson Nicoll, the editor of the *British Weekly*, felt that Dale's position was untenable. In a letter to the Scottish theologian James Denney, he wrote:

> I do not think [the view of Dale and White is one] for which any serious person will stand up in the future, though no one can say that it is impossible for God to annihilate a soul. However, these men see the obvious fact that Christ sees in the future energetic beings blessed or cursed. The thought of their not existing in the future seems never to have crossed his mind ... If Christ were to come now and preach a Gospel of immortality, while acknowledging that there was nothing to fear in death save extinction, I doubt if he would appeal to everyone ... There is a kind of spiritual fatigue among many people now that makes the thought of extinction not unwelcome'[20]

4. His understanding of the atonement

I have noted three areas of theological weakness in Dale. Where he was strongest was where he made his greatest contribution. When in 1875 he was invited to deliver the Congregational Lectures, he chose the atonement as his theme. For some time, Dale had been concerned for the tendency of many to see the atonement in a highly subjective way, as simply a demonstration of God's love. He was also concerned about the shift in theology away from the atonement as the centre of salvation, to the incarnation. This was evident in Broad Church Anglican thinking influenced by F. D. Maurice, but also among Nonconformists such as the principal of Spring Hill College, John Simon. In the lectures, Dale sought to restate the doctrine of the atonement as a substitutionary sacrifice, avoiding the commercial terminology of some older theologians, but also the subjectivism and moralism of some contemporary theologians. Overall it was a successful effort, whatever one's reservations at some points. Dale had a strong doctrine of God's wrath and the need for propitiation. He emphasized how in Christ God himself deals with his own wrath against sin. Christ is the propitiation for our sins.[21] That was the theme of an 1885 address before the London Missionary Society. For Dale, the atonement as a propitiation for sins was fundamental for missions.[22]

Dale's work on the atonement was a harbinger of a more conservative theological movement in Nonconformity in the early twentieth century. Most notably, P. T. Forsyth would take up the theme of the atonement in a number of works. However like Dale, Forsyth was hampered by his defective view of the Bible. That is really the tragedy of Dale. Had he not succumbed to the wily charms of higher criticism he might have been a far more constructive theologian.

2. Dale's critique of the old evangelicalism

Dale was critical of the old evangelicalism in which he had been brought up, and that was exemplified by James. In particular he was critical of the individualism of the spirituality of old evangelicalism. The old evangelicalism, wrote Dale,

> cared nothing for building up ideal churches, or for creating an ideal social order; it did not care much for any development of personal life and character which was not necessary to make sure of eternal blessedness and to augment it; it cared very little for any truth that had not a direct relation to salvation. What it cared for was to save individual men from eternal death. This done, Evangelicalism was apt to assume that everything would come right with them either in this world or the next.[23]

While Dale believed passionately in personal conversion, he also believed that the older evangelicalism had neglected the corporate and social dimensions of Christianity. In a sense Dale was returning to an older Puritan way of thinking of the Christian life. He was in fact a high church Congregationalist. He believed that, faced with the challenge of Puseyism and Rome, only such a position was tenable. Significantly, he wrote some excellent pieces on the nature and practice of Congregationalism, a handbook for church members and several historical studies. One of the weaknesses he felt of the older evangelicalism was its minimizing of the church in the Christian life. He wrote that the 'Evangelical movement encouraged what is called an undenominational temper. It emphasized the vital importance of the evangelical creed, but it regarded almost with indifference all forms of church polity that were not in apparent and irreconcilable antagonism to that creed'.[24] He was also critical of the older evangelicalism's withdrawal from the world, lack of concern for social transformation, indifference to politics and negative worldliness.

Dale made some valid points about the older evangelicalism that are as germane today. In particular what he said about the individualism of so much evangelical life and the indifference to the church is something that contemporary evangelicalism needs to hear. Evangelical churches can become spiritual

supermarkets where people pick and choose what they want
and ministries are developed to meet the demands of the mar-
ket. Like Dale we need to rediscover the idea of the church as a
covenanted community of God's redeemed people.

3. Dale's understanding of the Christian ministry

There was both continuity and discontinuity with the older
evangelicalism in Dale's understanding of the Christian ministry. Like James, he understood that his primary duty as a
minister was to preach the word to his congregation. Insofar as
he could with a large city centre congregation, Dale faithfully
pastored his people much as James had done. However there
was discontinuity as well. Whereas James saw evangelism and
the conversion of men and women as the supreme object of
his ministry, Dale saw things differently. He believed that the
pastor's chief responsibility was to pastor his flock by teaching
them the truth. He was critical at this point of James's idea
of earnestness and questioned whether it was possible to sus-
tain that in a long pastorate. He wrote: 'It is not possible — it
is not desirable — that you should always preach under the
strain of that agony of earnestness with which I trust you will be
sometimes inspired'.[25] Rather, ministers must apply themselves
to the hard work of teaching the faith and not only preaching evangelistic sermons. When someone heard that Dale was
preaching rigorously doctrinal sermons at Carr's Lane, he said
that the people would not stand it. 'They will have to stand
it', was Dale's stern reply and they did. Yet Dale was also an
evangelist. Indeed he said that every sermon 'should have a
relation more or less direct to the rescue of the world from sin
and its restoration to God'.[26] He could preach passionately for
the conversion of souls. He worked hard to reach the people of
Birmingham with the gospel. However he did not feel that this
was his primary gift. There was also a diversity of gifts among
ministers and Dale felt that it was wrong to force everyone into
the role of being evangelists. He recognized some men as specially gifted as evangelists and enthusiastically supported the
missions of D. L. Moody.

In their preaching, Dale believed that ministers had to address the great intellectual issues of the day. In his Yale Lectures on preaching, he urged aspiring preachers to commit themselves to deep study so that they could do this. He did not doubt that many would have their own intellectual struggles and that they would not be able to find answers to all their questions. What unanswered questions they had were not to be carried into the pulpit. There they were to preach the great central truths of the evangelical faith with passion and boldness. But even more than the intellectual issues, Dale felt that people needed ethical and moral instruction.[27] He felt a great responsibility for equipping his congregation so that they could live as Christians in the world. He was critical again of the older evangelicalism for its other-worldliness that often meant that Christians behaved and thought differently from other people. He sought to cultivate what he called a 'Christian worldliness'. He urged, for example, that his people get involved in municipal politics and see it as part of their Christian calling.

When challenged that there would be no politics in heaven, he replied:

> No politics in heaven! Well I suppose not; but there are no agricultural labourers there living on twelve shillings a week … there are no hereditary paupers there … there are no gaols … to which little children … are sent for an offence committed in ignorance … no unjust wars to be prevented … Politics un-Christian! … by going on the Boards of Works and Town Councils, and improving the drainage of great towns, and removing the causes of fever, men are but following Christ's footsteps.[28]

Through his preaching and lectures, he sought to relate the gospel to public and private life. Several of his books are collections of sermons and addresses along this line, the best known of which is *Laws of Christ for Common Life*.[29] Here he dealt with subjects such as property, business as a calling, business ethics, anger, cheerfulness, truth-telling, parties, holidays and exercise.

Dale did not think that a minister should be directly involved in politics, although he may be very active in the community, as he himself was. He sat on various municipal committees for education, sanitation, poor relief and so on. Dale did not hide his political Liberalism, though unlike Joseph Parker he did not preach it. But he did speak out on a range of public issues — for example, Irish Home Rule, the Eastern Question, and education.

We can see then that Dale developed a different understanding of ministry from that of James. At its heart they shared the same priorities, but Dale had a much more expansive understanding of the minister's role in society. Again it is arguable that he was reviving an older Puritan understanding of ministry that placed a greater emphasis on its social dimension.

One other area where Dale and James shared a common interest, but came to different conclusions, was in relation to theological education. Both took an intense interest in Spring Hill College and sat on its board. Initially, Dale shared James's view that ministerial education should be kept separate from university education. However, over time, Dale changed his view. By the 1880s, he was encouraging the college to relocate to Oxford, which it did in 1889 with the name Mansfield College. Dale had come to believe that Nonconformists needed to be at the heart of intellectual life. Ironically this move in many ways symbolized the movement of Nonconformity towards the cultural centre of English life with the long-term effect of diminishing its dissident ethos.

Dale is something of an enigma and nowhere more so than in his theology. On the one hand, he passionately believed and preached the central truths of the faith, upheld justification by faith alone and defended the doctrine of the substitutionary atonement. Yet he made a number of theological concessions that compromised his orthodoxy and contributed to the theological decay of Nonconformity. He felt deeply the intellectual challenges arising from the Victorian Crisis of Faith and felt duty-bound to meet them. The evangelical faith had to be rethought and restated in the modern world. I think he was right in his intention, but sadly conceded too much. His contemporary,

Spurgeon, conceded nothing, but sadly did not try to engage with the ideas of his times or encourage others to do so. As a result I think that he left the evangelical cause weaker and in his way contributed to the decline of Nonconformity. The tragedy was that there was not someone who combined Spurgeon's passion and orthodoxy with Dale's passion and intellectual ability. Nonconformity needed its Abraham Kuyper minus his Dutch idiosyncrasies, or a more popular B. B. Warfield or J. Gresham Machen. At least it needed men such as the latter who would support others in the pulpits. I think that Dale, like so many of his generation, was simply overwhelmed by the intellectual challenges of the times and gave way too easily. With hindsight, we can see that they were wrong and Spurgeon was right, but at the time it did not appear as clear cut as that. In assessing Dale, we need to be generous even as we recognize where he went wrong. Perhaps what Spurgeon said of Dale's commentary on Hebrews is the best assessment of Dale himself: 'Daring and bold in thought, and yet for the most part on the side of orthodoxy, his work commands the appreciation of cultured minds'.[30]

* * *

When Dale died in 1895 it was thought that no one could be found to take his place. When J. H. Jowett was called to the pastorate at Carr's Lane, he felt somewhat overwhelmed by the task. In the event, he maintained Carr's Lane as one of the flagships of Congregationalism during his sixteen year pastorate. Jowett was born and raised in Halifax, where his family worshipped at the Square Congregational Chapel. The pastor was the Enoch Mellor who was one of the leaders of the denomination and a conservative defender of the faith. Early on, Mellor identified young Jowett's potential and encouraged him to think of entering the ministry. When Jowett felt called to the ministry, he chose Airedale College for training. The principal was A. M. Fairbairn, who later became the first principal of Mansfield College. Fairbairn had studied in Germany and was a devotee of Wellhausen. At Airedale he encouraged higher critical study of the Bible. More radical than Fairbairn was Archibald Duff who taught Old Testament. He was very popular with the students and had a very formative influence on Jowett. After study at Edinburgh University, Jowett accepted a pastorate in Newcastle, from where he was called to Carr's Lane. During his time there, Jowett maintained the chapel as a preaching centre, but also transformed it into an institutional church, a lecture hall, cinema, café, billiard room and much else. This approach to church life became increasingly common among Congregationalists as a way of reaching the unreached people in their communities. After sixteen years, Jowett was called to Fifth Avenue Presbyterian church in New York. Such was his prominence that before he left he had tea with King George and Queen Mary. After five years there he accepted a call to Westminster Chapel, but not before a petition signed by, among many others, President Woodrow Wilson asked him to reconsider. His ministry at Westminster, where he succeeded Campbell Morgan, was dogged by ill health and he had to retire in 1922, dying the following year.

Theologically, Jowett was a liberal, although that was not always obvious from his preaching. His preaching was positive and uplifting in tone, intended to encourage, and concentrated on the theme of God's grace. He considered himself a broad evangelical. He did not believe in an inerrant Bible, although one would not have guessed it from his preaching. Critical issues were never mentioned from the pulpit. The trouble was that such preaching was dishonest. It had about it an air of unreality. The extent of Jowett's liberalism can be seen in a comment he made to a friend during the New Theology controversy in 1906. R. J. Campbell, Parker's successor at the City Temple, gave a lecture and then published a book in which he advanced a pantheist version of Christianity in which there was no fundamental distinction between God and humanity. Needless to say, a whole raft of basic Christian doctrines was denied. While others such as P. T. Forsyth engaged in battle, Jowett did not. He told a friend that he agreed with eleven-twelfths of what Campbell taught, the twelfth being Campbell's view of Christ and sin.

Jowett is symptomatic as to why Nonconformity declined theologically and as a spiritual force. In one of his last sermons he put in words the delusion by which Nonconformity was led down the dead end of liberalism.

> I believe that we are entering upon a day when we shall encounter many new terminologies. Men will be saying old things in new words. They will be giving new expressions to old truths. I plead that we never let a new phraseology frighten us into a sense of spiritual bereavement. Let us look very reverently and expectantly at the new presence, and we may find that in the very moment when we are tempted to think that we are pathetically bereaved we are face to face with the risen Lord and in open communion with his grace.[31]

That proved a vain hope, as the history of much twentieth-century Nonconformity bears witness. Contrary to what Dale, Jowett and many other Nonconformists believed, we cannot separate our experience of Christ from Scripture. If we do so, we will eventually lose Christ and find ourselves drifting doctrinally and spiritually. This is what happened in subsequent generations of Nonconformists. For those brought up in Nonconformity, there was not only no reason to be Nonconformists but no reason to be Christians. What was eventually lost, with the acceptance of a fallible Bible, was the gospel itself, without which Nonconformity is meaningless.

Happily all was not lost. Not at Carr's Lane, but elsewhere there were those who held fast to the faith. Before and after Jowett at Westminster Chapel, G. Campbell Morgan exercised a powerful ministry that took the Bible seriously. Of course, Campbell Morgan's colleague during the last years of his ministry and successor was Dr. D. Martyn Lloyd-Jones, whose ministry was the antithesis of what Nonconformity had become since the late nineteenth century. Through much of the twentieth century, evangelical Nonconformity was very weak, but today there are around the country many Nonconformist churches where the Word is faithfully preached and people come to know God and Jesus Christ whom he has sent. Evangelical Nonconformity is much reduced in numbers and influence compared to what it was in the nineteenth century, but the light of the gospel is still shining in hope that in years to come it will shine brighter still.

Chapter 6
Nonconformist Anglicans?
Melvin Tinker

Introduction

I am sure that it is not without significance that the title I have
been given for this talk, 'Nonconformist Anglicans' is followed
by a question mark. For some, it would appear to be an ox-
ymoron, a contradiction in terms. But this depends, I guess,
upon one's understanding of what constitutes nonconformity.
Some would, no doubt, hold the view that simply belonging to
the Church of England entails such compromise, in both theology and practice, that the term 'nonconformist' is an ill-fitting
one. Perhaps if we were to take the term in a strictly historical
sense — to describe the position of those who do not conform
to the doctrine and practices of the Established Church — then
yes, it is a self-contradictory term. However, we could broaden
the term, and apply it within an Established Church setting —
maybe conceiving the term judicially rather than historically,
to describe those who do not adhere to canon law or strictly
use the liturgy of the denomination. That would then entail
almost every clergyman in the Church of England being a nonconformist, for it is highly likely that very few, whatever their
theological stripe, follow the canons to the letter.

But if we were to consider nonconformity as a theological
principle, then it could be maintained that every true Bible-
believing Christian is a nonconformist. The principle is set out
for us by the apostle Paul in Romans 12:1:

> Therefore, I urge you, brothers, in view of God's mercy,
> to offer your bodies as living sacrifices, holy and pleas-
> ing to God — this is your spiritual worship. Do not con-
> form to the pattern of this world, but be transformed by
> the renewing of your mind. Then you will be able to test
> and approve what God's will is — his good, pleasing
> and acceptable will.

This call for the Christian to be nonconformist applies at every
point where a world in rebellion against its Maker impinges
upon his life. This includes the manifestation of that rebellion
within the church — at the local level of the congregation, as
well as at the wider national or international level of an association of churches. In other words, theologically, nonconformity
can be understood as a necessary stance against worldliness in
all its forms. Without it, the Christian and the church become
captive to Babylon and ineffective in Gospel witness. I would
want to argue that nonconformity is a relative term, such that,
paradoxically, there has to be a conforming nonconformity for
the sake of the gospel. Let me explain.

A gospel requirement

First, it has to be said that nonconformity in this sense is a
gospel requirement. The most obvious example of this is in the
book of Acts — specifically, in Peter's statement to the religious
authorities of his day, as we find it recorded in verse 29 of
chapter 5: 'We must obey God rather than men!' When limita-
tions are being imposed on the work of the gospel, a stance
of nonconformity must be taken. But more positively, we see
a case being made for what I call conforming nonconformity
by the apostle Paul in 1 Corinthians 9. In verse 12, we read of
the apostle Paul applying a policy of nonconformity to the right
to receive payment for his ministry (which the other apostles
claimed). And this, he says, was for the sake of the gospel, so,
as he puts it in verse 18, 'that in preaching the Gospel I may
offer it free of charge, and so not make use of my rights in
preaching it.'

But then Paul moves on to speak of a conforming which makes him a nonconformist:

> Though I am free and belong to no man, I make myself a slave to everyone, to win as many as possible. To the Jews I became like a Jew, to win Jews. To those under the law I became like one under the law. To those not having the law (though I am not free from God's law but am under Christ's law), so as to win those not having the law. To the weak I became weak, to win the weak. I have become all things to all men so that by all possible means I might save some. I do all this for the sake of the Gospel that I may share in its blessings (1 Cor. 9:19-23).

This is where the relativizing comes in. By conforming to the practices of one group, Paul becomes a nonconformist to another group, but only so as to conform to the requirements of the gospel so that some might be saved. Hence, conforming Non-conformity. But throughout it all it is his faithfulness to the gospel and his desire to win as many as possible that shapes and enables Paul's practice. So in some situations, he will conform as much as the most fervent reactionary — eating kosher food, all for the gospel's sake. In other situations he will appear loose and radical, even eating food sacrificed to idols, but not if it will cause a fellow believer to stumble — then he will appear reactionary again.

What we see in the practice of Paul is an outworking of the maintenance of the balance between *faithfulness* and *flexibility*: faithfulness to the unchanging truths of the gospel, which is not to be accommodated, assimilated or abandoned for the sake of fashion and ease, and yet, at the same time, flexibility in practices which enable that gospel to be communicated effectively. Walking that tightrope is not easy and will invariably mean being misunderstood and abused by friend and foe alike, as Paul knew to his own cost.

The church is easily drawn towards the one or the other extreme. On the one hand, there is the adoption of what the sociologist Peter Berger calls *cognitive and cultural resistance.* Here, the biblical call to flee from the world leads to a cultural isolation from the world, as we form our own sub-culture with its own conformity to traditions and patterns. These may owe more to a fear of contamination than to any gospel requirement. Thereby the freedom we have in Christ is compromised and gospel engagement is seriously curtailed. At the other extreme is *cognitive and cultural adaptation.* At this juncture, the church simply apes the world, dressing non-Christian ideas in thinly veiled Christian guise. It is simply assumed that 'Trad is bad and the latest is the greatest.' This not only applies to the more obvious influences of feminism and the gay movement upon church policy and practice, but also to the more acceptable vices such as the use of marketing and managerial techniques. The result is that it is these, rather than the gospel, which drive the agendas of many professing evangelical churches.

The third way is that exemplified by Paul which is *cognitive and cultural negotiation,* holding firm to the faith delivered once and for all to the saints and being flexible in how this is expressed, as any missionary worth his salt must be. To go down the one route leads to cultural isolation, and to go down the other involves cultural assimilation. Paul's way brings us into gospel engagement. As we shall see, this is the path many Anglican evangelicals are trying to tread, which makes them, by definition, nonconformist.

Historical precedent

Secondly, there is good historical precedent for what Anglican evangelicals are doing today. As far as was possible, Whitefield and the Wesleys did try to operate within the framework of the Established Church, but nonetheless engaged in irregular, though not strictly illegal, practices such as field preaching. What made this irregular was that it took place in other clergy's parishes. But for the sake of the gospel these men were willing to think 'outside the box' so that the gospel could be promoted. Other examples would include the use of lay preachers, the forming of societies and lectureships, and proprietary chapels.

Practical necessity

Thirdly, there is an increased practical necessity for Anglican nonconformity. This relates to the state of the Anglican denomination, as well as to the spiritual needs of our country.

The denomination is in a state of meltdown. All the figures, let alone some of the current trends, indicate this. In 1871, there were twenty-seven bishops and 20,609 clergy. Now there are 114 bishops and 9,500 stipendiary clergy. The number of bishops has more than quadrupled and the number of clergy more than halved. It is estimated that, over the next ten years, there will be a ten per cent reduction in the number of those entering the ordained ministry. When you add to that the fact that more women are being ordained, and that the average age for ordination is going up (it is now above forty), the future does not bode well for church growth. During the 1990s, there was a twenty-three per cent decline in church attendance in the Church of England. The only positive statistic is that there was a small growth of two per cent amongst those who labelled themselves 'evangelical'. When this category was broken down further, it was revealed that while those describing themselves as 'charismatic' evangelicals declined by twenty-one per cent, and 'broad evangelicals' by twenty-three per cent, mainstream evangelicals grew by an amazing three hundred per cent. Even so, together, such 'evangelicals' make up only twenty-four per cent of the entire Church of England.

As David Mills from the United States has shown, any collapsing organization tends to engage in five responses, which we are presently witnessing around the world: denial, centralization, homogenization, frantic activity and cleansing.[1] First, there is a denial that there is any crisis, as previous beliefs and practices begin to be jettisoned. This is simply a refusal to face the awful reality. It is a pretence that nothing has really changed. This is when such slogans as 'unity in diversity' are appealed to, in order to keep people on board. This is followed by increased centralization. The institution begins to collapse around the edges. Those located there are the first to recognize the problems and threaten to leave. Therefore it is much safer to rein things in, to keep things safe from such people. This way the institutional leaders gain more power for themselves. The training and distribution of clergy comes more into the hands of the bishops, as well, of course, as the money needed to finance such schemes. Thirdly, the collapsing institutions begin to homogenize themselves, hoping to eliminate differences and dissidents. They promote company men — those who can be all-embracing, except of course, for embracing evangelicals. And so attempts are made to change the way in which ordinands are trained at distinctive theological colleges — with moves to restrict the choice of colleges for ordinands, to 'broaden out' the more clearly evangelical colleges, and to appoint to senior positions so-called evangelicals who are Anglicans first and evangelicals second. Then there follows a period of frantic activity, not only to distract from the impending crisis but to get everyone pulling together, so as to foster the illusion that we are all on the same side. There will be diocesan youth events, calls for churches to work together for 'mission', the use of parish audits, and so on. But, when all else fails, the organization will try and expel the more divisive of its members in the hope that some sort of unity and control will be re-established.

In these circumstances, nonconformity is going to be a necessity to preserve the purity and practice of the gospel. Those committed to ministering within the Church of England, who believe they are the heirs of the Reformation and true to its title deeds, will seek, under God, to bring about change for the gospel's sake. In such a situation as I have described, three responses are open to evangelicals. These are options which present themselves to any organization in trouble, as shown by Robert Quinn in his book *Deep Change.*[2] There are those who engage in 'peace with pay': they keep their heads down and hope that things will keep together until their retirement, or maybe, hoping against hope, that things will only get better. Then there are those who make a quick exit and simply leave the organization. The third option is in line with the kind of nonconformity we have been looking at. That is to effect 'deep change'. This means caring enough to confront the issues. It entails breaking the rules, risking jobs and moving forward into an uncertain future, not quite knowing what the end game will be. Strategies and practices will be adopted which, it is believed, will promote the work of the gospel.

Present practice

I now want to outline some of these practices which are presently taking place and then go on to speak of future possibilities.

First, there is the issue of dress. Taking Paul's principle of 1 Corinthians 9, we have to work through what will assist and what will hinder the communication of the gospel. This involves more than simply being careful about the words we use and the style we adopt. It also affects the appearance of the ministers. Many do what we are doing at St John's, and have a flexible dress code. For the traditional 8 a.m. Book of Common Prayer service, which is mainly made up of older members, we adopt traditional dress — cassock, surplice and scarf. Not to do so would provide unnecessary offence — and in my view dress is a matter of indifference anyway. By way of contrast, for our major services — when we seek to engage with folk who are not from a church culture — we adopt smart but non-liturgical dress. Some wear clerical collar as a concession, as well as providing a helpful means of identification when you have a number of ministers on the staff. Others have abandoned any sign of clericalism altogether. But note again what the motivation is — to win some for Christ.

Secondly, there is increased flexibility and nonconformity with regards to liturgy. Many of us are convinced of the value of liturgy, but again only insofar as it will serve the gospel by edifying the saints. Much modern Anglican liturgy is, to be frank, liberal-catholic and light years from the theology of the Prayer Book. So this we will not use. We use a form of communion service based on the prayer book but in modern English, as well as our own devised baptism services. We also provide for variety in our non-sacramental services, using prayers, confessions, creeds and so on. These will assist in reinforcing the theme of the service, which in turn is determined by the Bible passage being expounded. Many churches do not follow the set readings — the lectionary — because they do not assist in systematic, well-rounded Bible exposition, nor are they sensitive to the needs of local congregations. Those needs have to be determined by the local leadership and responded to accordingly. For evangelistic guest services, liturgy is dropped altogether; a minimalist approach is adopted, so as to enable our non-church guests to feel comfortable in the right sense — so that, under the power of the Word, they are enabled to become uncomfortable in the right sense too.

Essential to the centralization that has been taking place is centralized funding. It is interesting to note that, while the central bodies may not care much for evangelical theology, they are very keen on raking in evangelical money! The financial crisis in the Church of England is one significant factor which is bringing deeper issues to a head. At one time, many clergy stipends were significantly supported by the central Church Commissioners, and supplemented by local congregational giving. In the 1980s, losses were incurred by the Commissioners totalling £800 million. A decision was taken to increase pension contributions, and in recent years a large number of clergy have come up for retirement. When you add to this declining congregations, the result is a financial crisis of major proportions. Chelmsford has a deficit of £600 thousand; Durham, £427 thousand; London, £1.1 million.

Consequently the local churches have been asked to provide more. This is achieved through a system known as the 'Parish Share' or 'Quota'. In theory, this is a voluntary contribution. Roughly speaking, the larger the congregation and the higher the income, the more one is expected to contribute to the central pot, regardless of how many clergy that church has. This is then shared out. There are no prizes for guessing which churches are being asked to contribute the most — evangelical ones, because they are the churches which tend to be growing and have good Christian giving. Many evangelical churches believe that on principle such a system is wrong and have decided to 'cap' their quota. The view is that they should pay for the cost of clergy, plus a contribution to the running costs of the diocese (administration, etc.), and no more. Given that many members are giving in good faith towards what they believe is gospel work, then that money should not go towards funding those who are undermining that work or are not actively forwarding it. That would be a breach of trust.

Churches such as these are still very charitable. They give large sums to overseas mission, as well as to home mission, but it is they, not a remote centre, who decide where the money goes. This would not be so necessary if those in positions of responsibility were doing their job properly. The bottom line is that it is absurd, if not downright criminal, to use evangelical money to prop up a liberal agenda. This is what makes the powers-that-be angry, and sometimes vindictive. Attempts are made to blackmail such congregations: 'You are causing the poorer churches to suffer because they cannot afford a minister', without thinking that they have some responsibility themselves in the matter, having adopted policies and appointed people who foster decline through apostasy. Then there are more direct threats: 'When this minister leaves, he will not be replaced until the quota is paid in full.'

Maybe there is something of a parallel with Luther at this point. As we know, the Roman Catholic Church in the fifteenth and sixteenth centuries embraced a wide variety of theological views, even allowing for those like Luther who believed in justification by faith alone. Theological debate was allowed and even encouraged. But when Luther worked through at the practical level the implications of indulgences, and thereby effectively cut off a vital source of revenue for the building of St Peter's Basilica, then he had to be challenged. Of course, there were other factors as well, but this was certainly a major one. Similarly, the Church of England hierarchy can make all sorts of noises about being 'all-embracing' and appreciating the contribution of the 'evangelical tradition', especially in its zeal for mission, but once evangelical belief starts to bite on the hard reality of money — which means power — then their true views of us are exposed.

With the rise of more and more 'open' heretical bishops, some churches have declared 'impaired communion'. That is, while recognizing that the Bishop has certain legal rights and responsibilities, his views forfeit his right to exercise spiritual oversight. Some have invited overseas bishops to perform con- . firmations. This has implications for the future which we shall mention shortly.

Two other important areas are the training and deployment of ministers, and, linked to this, church planting. Many churches are having to think beyond the 'ordained' ministry in order to promote gospel work. The old system of maybe a vicar and a curate is no longer sufficient if we are going to engage effectively in mission. People need to be raised up, under God, and provided training for coalface gospel ministry. A number of churches have adopted apprenticeship schemes, whereby young men and women are taken on by a church (some of them funding themselves) to undergo practical training and receive theological instruction. We have a number of folk on what is called a Ministerial Training Scheme (MTS). They come to us for two years; someone is assigned to oversee their work; they are given duties to perform within the church; they receive a book grant and are sent on one day a week to the Cornhill training scheme. They have hands-on experience of ministry, are given good critical feedback, and pick up, by being part of a team, the strategy and vision-making which shapes evangelical ministry. Some of these people come from elsewhere; others are 'home-grown'. Some then go on to ordination, while others find other suitable forms of Christian ministry; still others may go into secular employment, but will have acquired skills which will be a blessing to any church. It also provides a good sifting ground, so that some can test their gifts under supervision and then, after a year, if it is clear that for whatever reason they are not suitable, they can be released without too great a cost. What is nonconformist about this is that such people are taken on by the local church and are commissioned by the local church, not by the Bishop. They are not officially licensed and they do not go through a Diocesan training scheme, which by and large are designed to produce liberals.

This ties in to another important development — church planting. To some extent this is no longer so radical. Church planting is now considered kosher and a 'good thing'. Therefore, it is not difficult to get Diocesan support, especially when things are so desperate. It is relatively easy to get support for planting within one's own parish. The difficulty comes when plans are made to plant in someone else's parish! In some cases this is possible. A 'transplant' may take place, whereby a dead church building is taken over and a new congregation meets there with a new minister, both of which come from the planting parish. What is not so easy is when a local non-evangelical clergyman objects. Bishops are too weak-willed to do anything about it, and so give in to the status quo. What options are there? The first choice is to go ahead anyway and see what happens. Second, an option is to designate the new church plant as non-Anglican, but sponsored by a local Anglican church. This enables the church to be outside Episcopal control, but to have the oversight of the mother church; so, in effect, it is Anglican in all but name. Thirdly, as is happening in Manchester at the moment, the church plant can be a missionary church, and so come under an Anglican missionary organization like Crosslinks. This means it is not a parish church, but a missionary Anglican one. One can still ask the Bishop for a licence, but if it is not given one can still minister as an ordained Anglican, but irregularly.

Again let me be at pains to point out that all such ventures are not being undertaken because we want to be angular and difficult, but because of our commitment to the gospel. So we will be nonconformist conformists!

Future possibilities

I mentioned earlier the need to effect 'deep change'; this involves moving ahead into an uncertain future, or building bridges while still crossing them. Therefore, it is difficult to predict with any accuracy how the future will develop. But let me mention a few possibilities based upon our present trajectory, with the qualification that I am neither a prophet nor a son of a prophet.

One thing which may happen as a result of the international Anglican scene is a realignment of churches. There is no reason in principle why the focus for a new worldwide Anglicanism should not shift to, say, Sydney or Singapore, or to any other city which holds and promotes orthodoxy, rather than Canterbury. The present arrangement is a matter of history that can be changed. The result in this country may be a parallel Anglican denomination, similar to the position in South Africa.

Certainly, the issue of selection and training of ordained ministers and their deployment has to be given serious thought. We cannot allow evangelical ministry to be stymied at the selection level — with good people being refused because of doctrine or because of financial pressure — nor can we allow their training to be compromised by regional schemes which force colleges to become more latitudinarian. Thinking and discussion need to be going on now to secure the future.

I would hope that if such developments occur, there will be a move in the direction of the practice of the magisterial Reformers, whereby other people's ministry is recognized and an interchange takes place. Those who are not Episcopally ordained but are in good standing in faith and practice should be received by churches which practise Episcopal ordination, and vice versa. This would also allow for greater fluidity in ministries where church planting is undertaken in pioneering situations.

Conclusion

Whatever the shortcomings, frustrations and disappointments, nonconformity is alive and well within the Church of England. The same gospel which led faithful men into nonconformist ministry in the seventeenth century is the same gospel which is leading men into nonconformist ministry within the Church of England at the beginning of the twenty-first century. Our passion is for the lost. Our rule is God's Word. Our strength comes from God's Spirit. Our desire is to promote the glory of Christ to the praise of God the Father. Our faults are all our own.

Chapter 7
The Future of Nonconformity
Mark Johnston

Introduction

A number of years ago, a mobile phone advertising campaign that had flourished in England, Scotland and Wales, foundered in Northern Ireland. Its slogan was, 'The Future is Bright: the Future is *Orange!*' It was hardly designed to help a peace process in its infancy! The future may or may not be bright for the Orange network, or for the Ulster Peace Process, but the question for us is: just how bright is the future for the Nonconformist cause in Britain?

At face value, the answer to that question might seem to be, 'Not very!' Many chapel congregations are ageing and dwindling, Presbyterian denominations are fragmenting and losing influence and the hoped-for revival of Puritanism has not materialized. The situation is further complicated by the dramatic cultural shift experienced by this present generation. We have moved into an era dominated as never before by post-Enlightenment individualism. We are, it appears, left with a situation summed up by a minister who, bemoaning falling attendances at Nonconformist-type conferences, said, 'Let's face it, experimental Calvinism is no longer the flavour of the month!'

The current apparent decline raises questions at a number of levels. Do declining numbers mean that we must rethink our theology and strategy? Do we simply acknowledge the sovereignty of providence and go into pietistic bunker-mode? Or is it the case that we need to rethink the present situation facing churches, in light of both Scripture and the past? The answer can really only be the latter option. We need to rediscover and appreciate afresh our Nonconformist heritage as it relates to a new generation. That is certainly the line I want to pursue in the remainder of this chapter; but first we need to sketch in some background details.

A significant (though not the sole) factor in the evangelical recovery that took place in Britain during the last century was the rediscovery of the Puritans. It started with a group of Oxford and Cambridge students, including J. I. Packer and Raymond Johnston, who began meeting to explore Puritan literature as early as 1948. The group quickly found its focus in Westminster Chapel, under the guiding hand of Martyn Lloyd-Jones, and then grew from there into what was to become the Puritan Studies Conference. It was not a 'Nonconformist' group in the ecclesiastical sense, but it did embrace the spirit of Nonconformity. The growing strength and influence of this little movement was reflected in the establishment in 1957, and subsequent growth, of the Banner of Truth Trust with its different ministries. All this led to heightened expectations among a new generation of Christians.

However, the movement reached a major watershed in 1966 with the reaction to Dr Lloyd-Jones's address at the National Assembly of Evangelicals in Westminster Central Hall. The details of what was and was not said that night are in one sense immaterial; what is clear is that what happened that evening led to a significant parting of the ways over the issue of denominational alignment.

The decades that followed saw further fragmentation on both sides of the Anglican/ Nonconformist divide, over charismatic issues and the emergence of new churches. The development of the respective groupings since that time has to a large extent been reflected in the Banner of Truth and Proclamation Trusts for Nonconformist and Anglican evangelicals respectively and *Spring Harvest* and *Word Alive* for those with charismatic leanings.

What we want to do in the remainder of this chapter is to reflect on the essence of Nonconformity in its Puritan past, see how it is first and foremost a spirit that transcends denominations (it was born within Anglicanism), and then go on to argue that it has a vital role in the preservation of the gospel, in the fullest sense of the word, for the future.

The draft title given to this paper in the early stages of planning was, '*Is there a* future for Nonconformity?' I want to stick with the question in that title and answer it by saying, 'Yes! If...' — taking the line that the essence of Nonconformity lies in the Puritan movement of the sixteenth and seventeenth centuries and its spiritual legacy down to the present time. In light of what these men stood for and achieved, there is good reason to believe that there *is* a future for Nonconformity, if we grasp six important features of what the Puritans were and stood for.

1. If we appreciate the genius of Puritanism

When scanning through much of what has been written and said about the Puritans — even by evangelicals — it is plain to see they tend to get a pretty bad press. Indeed, the name 'Puritan' was originally intended as a smear from the start and it remains so for many to the present. In one sense it is not hard to pick out the faults, failings and inconsistencies in those who bore that name in the sixteenth and seventeenth centuries, and also in those who are their spiritual descendants; however, to major on that would be to overlook the outstanding achievements of this movement. Its theology and influence have in many ways long outlived the men who founded it.

J. I. Packer captures the significance and relevance of the Puritans by comparing them to the Giant Redwood trees of Northern California:

As Redwoods attract the eye, because they overtop other trees, so the mature holiness and fortitude of the great Puritans shine before us as a kind of beacon light, overtopping the stature of the majority of Christians in most eras, and certainly so in this age of crushing urban collectivism, when Western Christians sometimes feel and often look like ants on an anthill and puppets

> on a string ... In this situation the teaching and example
> of the Puritans has much to say to us.[1]

That leaves us wondering what, then, was the genius of Puritanism that gave it such far-reaching and enduring significance? We can single out five main characteristics that are worth noting:

1. Their view of God

Everything these men believed, were and stood for stemmed from their high view of God. (The same was true for their predecessors in the Reformation in Europe and England.) The point is well illustrated by the fact that the first derisory epithet attached to these men was 'Precisians' or 'Precisionists'. When Richard Rogers (a minister in Wetherfield, Essex) was asked by a gentleman what made him so precise, he responded, 'Oh, Sir, I serve a precise God!'

Straightaway, we can see what is going wrong in so many churches today: they embrace a view of God that has been dumbed down in the name of popular Christianity. Even as far back as the 1970s, Leith Samuel could say in the title of a book, *Your God is too Small!* The recovery of healthy, vibrant churches is bound up with the need to recover a high view of God.

2. Their esteem of Scripture

The Puritan regard for Scripture is nowhere expressed more succinctly than in question two of the *Westminster Shorter Catechism*:

> Q. What rule has God given to direct us how we
>   may glorify and enjoy him?
> A. The Word of God which is contained in the
>   Scriptures of the Old and New Testaments, is
>   the only rule to direct us how we may glorify
>   and enjoy him.

In making that formulation and locating it where they did in their catechism, these men were simply reiterating the principle of *sola scriptura* that lay at the heart of the Protestant Reformation, safeguarding the heart of both gospel and church.

The problem in our day is not merely that the revelation of Holy Scripture is rivalled by many other forms of revelation; but that also too often Scripture is subordinated to reason. If the spirit of Nonconformity is to survive, it must bow, neither to the temple of fresh revelation, nor to the academy, but to the Word of God alone.

3. Their understanding of salvation

It is commonplace in contemporary theology — at least at a popular level — to construe 'salvation' as 'the point of conversion'; but that is to lose sight of its larger biblical horizons. Thomas Manton gives us a glimpse of the full-orbed understanding of salvation that was typical of his Puritan counterparts and which shaped their view of the gospel:

> The sum of the gospel is this, that all who, by repentance and faith do forsake the flesh, the world and the devil, and give themselves up to Father, Son and Holy Spirit, as their creator, redeemer and sanctifier, shall find God as a father taking them for his reconciled children, and for Christ's sake pardoning their sin, and by his Spirit giving them his grace; and if they persevere in this course, will finally glorify them, and bestow upon them everlasting happiness.[2]

This larger understanding of salvation explains the Puritan use of the term 'regeneration' and their richer understanding of evangelism to which we will come back later. It also explains the disparity between present-day expectations regarding conversion and the way they are fulfilled, that stems from too narrow an understanding of salvation.

4. Their appreciation of the church

If there is one thing that can be identified as the main cata-
lyst for the emergence of the Puritans, it was their concern for
the reformation of the church. They had a high view of the
church. This first began to come to the fore in their criticisms
of the Elizabethan Settlement. Many of these young men were
Cambridge graduates, who entered the ministry of the Church
of England in order to press for ongoing reform at a congregational level.

We will come back to this in more detail later.The post-Enlightenment individualism that has become the hallmark of the
twenty-first century church has robbed us of that biblical view
that sees the church as the glorious body and radiant bride of
Christ — the doctrine of the church is really the Cinderella of
theology.

5. Their concern for the world as a whole

The fifth strand of Puritan distinctiveness worth highlighting
is its view of life and community as an integrated whole —
the Puritans believed that God has sanctioned the solidarity
of society. This translated into their vigorous (however
imperfect) efforts in the political sphere — reaching their
zenith in the Glorious Revolution and the establishment of
the Commonwealth. Even though Puritans differed among
themselves as to the nature of the relationship between church
and state, they held a generally shared conviction that the
church has a God-given role in the life of the community at
large that went beyond the need for evangelism. (This point is
helpfully explored in relation to the influence of the so-called
'High Calvinists' of the nineteenth century by Ian Shaw and is
illustrated also in nineteenth-century Scotland in the ministries
of Thomas Chalmers in Glasgow and Edinburgh.[3])

Reaction against the aberrations of what became known
as the 'social gospel' in the early part of the twentieth century
led in many cases to a neglect of wider social responsibility by
its end in many Nonconformist churches. Yet a significant part

of their Puritan heritage lies in a concern for God's truth to be applied to social and political concerns, enabling Christians to function as salt and light in a dark and putrefying world.

The problem with much of the Puritan renaissance that swept through Britain in the last half-century is that it has embraced only a Reformed/Puritan soteriology — one that fails to grasp the grandeur and integrity of the world-life view of our spiritual forebears. (Interestingly, that stands in contrast to the corresponding renaissance that has taken place in American churches.) If there is to be a future under God for Nonconformity in Britain, we need to appreciate afresh the genius of this movement from its earliest days.

2. If we cultivate the spirituality of the Puritans

'Spirituality' is one of the buzz-words of this present generation — it is only a pity that it has been brought back into our vocabulary by acolytes of New Age philosophy! That surely reflects on a century and more of evangelical spirituality that was and continues to be both truncated and myopic.

Through the holiness theology of the Keswick movement and its step-daughters in Pentecostal and charismatic theology, a whole new understanding of spirituality emerged — one that struggled to find biblically persuasive answers for the problems of sin, suffering and sanctification in the Christian life. Dr Packer probably speaks for many who have struggled with these influences — in light of their experience, as much as in their understanding of Scripture — when he says he only first began to find satisfaction in the Puritans. Again, there are a number of specific areas of their spirituality that are worth noting:

1. They took sin seriously

Ralph Venning says it all in the title of his book: *The Sinfulness of Sin*. These men were classically styled 'physicians of soul' and as such were concerned with an accurate diagnosis of the soul's deepest complaint. Far from seeing 'sin' as some vague classification that somehow was linked to man's being under

divine displeasure, they saw it in all its ugliness and seriousness. It was seen not merely as that deepest malaise of soul
that cuts us off from God and that can only be dealt with by the
grace of justification, but it was also seen as the running sore
of the Christian life that can only be dealt with by the grace of
sanctification.

The reason there is so much shallowness in much contemporary Christianity is that there is so little seriousness in the way
sin is viewed both from the pulpit and in the pew.

2. They lived in the shadow of death

Improvements in social conditions in the Western world today,
combined with the quality of health care available, mean that
people can expect — all things considered — to enjoy a long
life. The same cannot be said for those who lived in the sixteenth and seventeenth centuries. A very real sense of human
mortality and the brevity of our time in this world brought the
issues of death and life in the world to come into sharp focus for the Puritans and it affected their grasp of these central
themes in Scripture.

As we find ourselves living increasingly in a 'death-denying
culture', we need to encourage people not only to reckon with
the reality of death, but also to realize that 'a person is not
ready to live until they are ready to die.'

3. They had a holistic view of life

Another feature of life in the twenty-first century, to which we
would do well to apply some Puritan wisdom, is our atomistic
approach to life — an attitude that leads to a compartmental-
ized existence. This affects us as Christians, in that we all too
easily confine our understanding of spirituality to certain times
in our week and certain segments of our life — this explains a
great deal of spiritual dysfunction.

If Puritan spirituality can be captured in a single sentence,
then it must surely be in its best-known assertion: 'Man's chief
end is to glorify God and enjoy him forever!' The controlling

concern in Puritan Christianity was to know God truly and to serve him rightly — in the words of Peter Lewis, 'Puritanism was sainthood visible.'[4] The visibility of our faith needs to go far beyond the number of church meetings we attend and activities in which we are involved!

4. They saw all truth as being 'unto godliness'

Perhaps the greatest factor in the strength of Puritan spirituality was the way it was rooted in theology. Martyn Lloyd-Jones used to illustrate that in his ministry by pointing to the function of a building's steel frame — without it, the entire edifice could not stand!

Theology for our seventeenth-century spiritual forebears was never a merely academic exercise, but always a means by which to cultivate communion with God and to live increasingly to his glory. Add to this the fact that the Puritans saw this not as a privatized but a shared responsibility, and it is not hard to see that those who belonged to this movement stood out because of their lives.

Putting all this together, Packer argues that the Puritan approach to faith and life provides the antidote for three of the most troublesome groups of Christians in our time: *restless experientialists, entrenched intellectualists* and *disaffected deviationists.*[5] The need for a spirituality that is both God-glorifying and personally satisfying is paramount for the church in every generation: it needs to be rediscovered, not invented!

3. If we share the vision of the Puritans

As has been said already, the Puritan movement was born out of a concern to reform the Church of England. Even as it was both forced and moved by choice out of that church, its vision for ongoing reformation was at the heart of much of Puritan labour. This concern expressed itself in the pursuit of reform in three areas: worship, church order and church membership. These issues continue to be matters for discussion and debate in the church of our day and we ignore them at the church's peril. Let me offer just a few brief thoughts on each to show why they continue to be important:

1. The worship issue is bigger than we think

Almost the entire debate over worship in recent decades has been dominated by 'traditional' versus 'contemporary'; but there is a much deeper issue at stake. It is the issue of what God's people are doing when they meet together as the church.

One prominent Anglican evangelical's answer to that question is, 'We are *not* there to "worship" — we are just there to meet with Jesus!' the Puritans would have had something very different to say! There is not space to develop these thoughts here; but suffice it to say, our view of worship will profoundly affect the shape of our life as the people of God and the character of our witness to the world.

2. The need for reform must be faced by every generation

It was the seventeenth-century theologian Gisbert Voetius — a Dutch counterpart to the English Puritans — who coined the expression, 'The Church that is reformed must always be reforming.' He was not using the term 'reformed' in its narrow sense of being Calvinistic in theology and polity, but rather to describe the ongoing nature of saving transformation in the corporate life of the people of God. It was that vision that inspired the early Puritans within the Church of England. Many laboured to further that reform within that church until the day they died. (Far from being an anti-Anglican movement, Puritanism was seen as a 'cuckoo in the Anglican nest, in it but not really of it — and that from the beginning!'[6]).

The Westminster Assembly was called with the express purpose of seeking a basis of faith and a form of church government that would be more widely agreeable in Britain: its goal was ongoing ecclesiastical reform. The so-called 'Grand Debate' over church polity in the assembly did not find that consensus; however, even their disagreements were to prove fruitful for the church polity of the major groupings who were influenced by the Confession and Catechisms that it produced.

The task of ongoing reformation remains for every church in every age as it faces the challenge of the changing times we live in — to discharge this task is simply to be true to the spirit of Nonconformity.

3. The question of what it means to be a Christian is at the heart of what it means to be a church

Alongside the elimination of 'popery from the worship and prelacy in the government' of the Church of England, a major concern of Puritan reform was to remove 'pagan irreligion from its membership'.[7] That did not mean to say that the Puritans saw no place for the unconverted in their services, or that they did not seek to evangelize them; rather it revealed their understanding of what constituted the church. They saw it as the covenant community of the people of God. This is an issue that touches every church at the deepest possible level. Christ came into the world to save 'a people for himself' — a new community that would stand out for him as his counter-culture in a fallen world — that must be the vision for his people in every age!

4. If we hold the convictions of the Puritans

Out of all the many strengths of the Puritans, the strength of their convictions was one of their most defining characteristics — it was a mark of their utter devotion to God and to the gospel. It led to their being willing to take on kings and prelates in the pursuit of reform, to the drafting and signing of the Solemn League and Covenant in 1643 and their readiness to face persecution and imprisonment for the sake of their cause. However, the greatest example of the strength of their resolve was seen in the Great Ejection of 1662. Some two thousand Nonconformist ministers were ejected from their livings as a result.

The fact that so many men (and their families) were prepared to pay such a high price for the sake of conscience was
not, as some have suggested, due to a 'peevish humour', but
rather because of convictions that were moulded by Scripture
and a heartfelt desire for integrity. What they were required
to abjure and to swear by the 1662 Act of Uniformity would
have been a complete denial of what they had fought for over
the past century. Expediency could never be a good reason to
abandon such convictions held for so long, because the underlying issue at stake was that of the authority of Scripture.

In contemporary terms, this issue raises some painful questions: a mere glance over the past hundred years will reveal a
story of battles fought, divisions that followed and the cause
of Christ in what appears to be perpetual disintegration — it
is hard not to feel cynical. However, there are two things that
help to bring what is at stake into focus: one is the kind of issue
over which we must take a stand, and the other is the extent
to which we are to be bound by church courts. Each in its own
way is a sliding scale, but in both there is a line we cannot cross
over.

5. If we pursue the catholicity of the Puritans

In light of what have just considered about the Puritan conscience, it is easy to focus on debates about small things with
which they are associated — such as rings, vestments and fes-
tivals. There is no doubt that they were capable of robust and
vigorous debate! But at the same time, they were bound together by an extraordinary spirit of catholicity. The unity they
enjoyed transcended the boundaries of particular views on polity or doctrine.

The fact that the Westminster Assembly was comprised of
a highly diverse group of divines evidenced that it was no hin-
drance to achieving the most fruitful theological consensus.

It has been all too easy to divide along denominational
and party lines in our debates, when in fact the greater need
is to stand together on issues that cross those lines. The spirit

of Nonconformity is one that not only galvanizes convictions under Scripture, but under that same Scripture also tirelessly pursues the unity of the body of Christ visibly on earth.

6. If we proclaim the gospel of the Puritans

We have already seen that the Puritan view of salvation was much bigger than what is generally held today; that view of salvation affected their view of the gospel and how it should be proclaimed. These men preached a 'comprehensive gospel' — preaching not merely for people to 'say the words', but for evidence of conversion, in the marks of grace in people's lives.

Their gospel labours were grounded in the conviction that 'salvation is of the Lord'. In the words of Thomas Watson, 'Ministers knock at the door of men's hearts, the Spirit comes with a key and opens the door.'[8] It is clear from reading their evangelistic sermons and literature that their views on divine sovereignty were no obstacle to their preaching both with persuasion and with passion.

Too much of today's gospel and the means by which it is communicated is reductionist, programmatic and geared towards immediate results. If there is to be a future for Nonconformity, then it has to include a place for full-orbed gospel preaching that looks to God to give the increase to our labours.

Conclusion

It would not be hard to argue that the greatest and most enduring achievement of the Puritan era was the fruit of the Westminster Assembly. This is seen in the form of that set of documents it produced expressing a shared understanding of Scripture that transcends the boundaries of church polity. The assembly was called to create uniformity in the church in Britain that was based on consensus. It succeeded in part — witness the value and durability of the *Westminster Confession of Faith*, the *Savoy Declaration* and the *1689 Baptist Confession* — but it singularly failed in many other respects.

Over the past ten years there have been many indications that there is a renewed longing to find that kind of consensus — rooted in God and shaped by his word. And there has been no shortage of gatherings and initiatives to pursue it. Out of all those gatherings that I have had the privilege to attend, one comment has lingered on. We were discussing the need to work together for more meaningful theological and ecclesiastical ties between churches in Britain, when one delegate said, 'Brothers, we have it within our grasp to finish unfinished business of the seventeenth century!' It may sound like something of a pipe-dream, but that is the thought I would leave with you as we draw the threads of our deliberations to a conclusion.

The great danger we face in our day on all sides is that of splintering into an independency based on minimalist theology in which everyone does their own thing. If that proves to be the outcome, it will be a tragic loss to the evangelical cause in this country. If there is to be a positive future for Nonconformity it cannot be achieved without humble cooperation and a shared vision to pursue true reform in light of the teaching and application of 'the whole counsel of God'.

Epilogue

So where have all the Nonconformists gone?

For many evangelicals today, Nonconformity is a non-issue. They believe it makes no sense to discriminate between Anglican and Nonconformist churches, or to favour one over the other. Anecdotal evidence indicates that, increasingly, Nonconformists are taking a relaxed attitude to their Nonconformity. Students from Baptist or Independent congregations go off to university, and attend the evangelical Anglican church there. A family with young children move home, and decide to join the Anglican church in their new town. They see no problem at all with joining an evangelical Anglican church, in preference over the local Nonconformist congregation, if they believe that suits their own or their family's needs.

There are, indeed, a number of reasons why evangelicals today might prefer to join an evangelical Anglican church, rather than a Nonconformist meeting.

1. Evangelism

Anglican evangelical churches are often well organized for evangelism. They seem to have a ready ability to attract to their services people of all ages who do not normally go to church. An unbeliever in England may feel more comfortable going to an Anglican church than to a Nonconformist chapel. He may believe that he will feel less ill-at-ease in the national church than in some independent meeting-place with which he has no affinity or knowledge whatsoever. And evangelical Anglican churches often make a particular, sustained effort to make themselves welcoming to non-churchgoers — in the shape of their services, the language they use, their dress, and so on. There is perhaps also a sense that being part of the Established Church lends a certain legitimacy to evangelistic activities, which Nonconformist churches cannot have. These factors may influence an evangelical to choose an evangelical Anglican church over the local Nonconformist chapel.

2. Ethos

Evangelical Anglican churches often make a particular effort to be contemporary in their approach. The use of modern songs, a variety of instruments to accompany the singing and a relatively informal style of leading the services can all prove attractive. A strong sense of leadership and direction, with a clear sense of where the church is going and what it is seeking to do, can reinforce the feeling that this is a church to which it would be good to belong.

3. Teaching

An evangelical can expect to receive sound, biblical teaching, clearly explained, in many evangelical Anglican churches. He can expect not to be misled and to grow in his understanding of the faith. He can expect contemporary application and clear teaching on how to deal with the difficulties and challenges of Christian life in the twenty-first century. These are clearly very attractive features for an evangelical.

No doubt there are other reasons why a Nonconformist might choose to attend an Anglican church rather than a Nonconformist church. Certainly many do, even when there is a sound Nonconformist church in the same area.

So is there any problem with this? Should an evangelical Nonconformist think twice before deciding to attend an Anglican church? The advantages listed above are often real enough. If we can be part of an Anglican church with sound teaching, contemporary ethos and effective evangelism which attracts non-churchgoers, is there any reason, in fact, for Nonconformist churches to continue at all? Why perpetuate the divisions of the past? If we hold the fundamentals of the gospel in common (as we surely do), what possible objection could there be to attending an Anglican church rather than a Nonconformist one?

What, in essence, is the justification for Nonconformity today? This is the essential question which this book has sought to explore.

We have looked at the matter historically (in particular, in the chapters by Robert Oliver, Paul Cook and Ken Brownell). Our Nonconformist forebears would not have countenanced joining an Anglican church, however evangelical, though many of them remained on good terms with their evangelical Anglican brethren. For some, attendance at an Anglican service might have been a matter for church discipline. Their refusal to conform to Anglicanism debarred them from many privileges of ordinary life — public office, university education and even in some cases burial in the local cemetery. They had serious convictions on this matter, and their convictions were costly. Yet they clung to them.

This should make us think. Why were they so tenacious in their view? Clearly, they were not just being difficult. No, they believed that they had good scriptural grounds for separating themselves from Anglican communion. They believed that Christ, the Head of the church, has laid down principles in his Word, which teach the members of a local church how they are to organize and govern themselves. In other words, they believed that the Christian is to have a biblical doctrine of the local church. When they sought to test this against what they saw in the Anglican system, they reached the view that, in its organization and government, the Church of England fell seriously short of what Scripture requires. They therefore sought to establish local churches which followed Scriptural teaching, as they understood it, more closely.

Secondly then, and most importantly, the contributors to this book have sought to look at the matter, as our forebears did, biblically and doctrinally. Sadly, however, the biblical doctrine of the local church has for many years been very low on the agenda of evangelicals. We have rightly emphasized the biblical doctrine of salvation — how may a man be right with God? We have carefully guarded the vital biblical doctrines of justification and atonement. We have also been careful to maintain in our understanding and teaching the biblical doctrines of the full deity and full humanity of Christ, the attributes of God and the deity of the Holy Spirit. We have sought to maintain biblical principles in our daily lives — in our morality and ethics. But somehow the doctrine of the local church has been forgotten. It is time for it to be rediscovered and reemphasized. It needs again to be proclaimed from our pulpits. Christians again need to see its importance for their lives, and again learn to obey what Christ teaches in this vital area.

The principles that lie at the heart of the biblical doctrine of the local church, as the Nonconformist understands them, are expounded, with his customary clarity, in Stuart Olyott's chapter in this book. I would urge every reader to study them closely, Bible in hand, to see whether that is indeed what Christ teaches in his Word. And if it is, as I firmly believe to be so, then we should have the courage and conviction to obey Christ in that area of our lives as well, at whatever cost to our comfort and personal preferences.

The Nonconformist's conscience is, or should be, utterly captive to the Word of God. He believes that Scripture does set out a pattern for the government of the local church — that a local church is in essence a gathered community of believers who commit themselves one to another to serve Christ and one another together, in the bonds of the gospel; that it is governed by elders and deacons, with no oversight from diocesan bishops or other dignitaries; and that the state is not to concern itself with or interfere in spiritual matters which are the concern of the church. While he regards his evangelical Anglican brothers and sisters with true Christian love, and desires their good in every way, he cannot, in good conscience, join with them in what he regards as a compromised and unscriptural national body, many of whose teachers teach doctrines which are utterly contrary to scriptural truth. Though his local Nonconformist church may not be all that it could or should be, yet he believes it to be founded on scriptural principles, and he will give himself to it without reserve, to the glory of Christ. He will attend its meetings, care for his fellow members, seek to win his friends for Christ, support his pastor and elders, and, in every way he can, participate fully in the life of the church.

In the Scriptures, Christ has surely given us a clear pattern for the local church. Do we dare follow any other?

Robert Strivens
London Theological Seminary

Notes

Chapter 1 — The Freedom of the Free Churchman

1. Michael R. Watts, *The Dissenters,* vol. 1, *From the Reformation to the French Revolution,* Oxford: Clarendon Press, 1978, p.1.
2. David M. Thompson, *Nonconformity in the Nineteenth Century,* Routledge and Kegan Paul, 1972, p.52.
3. Thomas Helwys, *The Mistery of Iniquity,* facsimile (1935), p.69. Quoted by N. H. Keeble in *The Literary Culture of Nonconformity in Later Seventeenth-Century England,* Leicester University Press, 1987, p.14.
4. Harry Blamires, *The Post-Christian Mind,* Vine Books, 1999, p.23.
5. Michael R. Watts, *The Dissenters,* vol. 2, *The Expansion of Evangelical Nonconformity, 1791-1859,* Oxford: Clarendon Press, 1995, pp.7, 68.
6. In a letter to John Mason, dated 13 January 1790, *Works,* vol. xii, p.455, quoted in *Journals,* ed. Nehemiah Curnock, vol. 8 (1916), p.37.
7. Michael R. Watts, *The Dissenters,* vol. 1, Oxford: Clarendon Press, 1978, p.220. R. Tudur Jones, commenting on the events of St Bartholomew's Day, 24 August 1662, 'So modern Nonconformity was born in England and Wales.' *Congregationalism in England 1662-1962,* London: Independent Press, 1962, p.59.
8. Quoted by B. R. White in *The English Separatist Tradition,* Oxford University Press, 1971, p.89.
9. George Whitefield, *Letters,* no. LXXXII.

10. Quoted by N. H. Keeble in *The Literary Culture of Non-conformity in Seventeenth-Century England,* Leicester University Press, 1987, p.191.
11. Ibid., p.202.
12. Ibid., p.152.
13. Which established the Civil Registry of Births, Marriages and Deaths.
14. For a number of seventeenth-century examples of this, see Diocese of Carlisle, Ecclesiastical Courts, Correction Court, Carlisle Record Office, DRC 5.
15. Michael R. Watts, *The Dissenters,* vol. 2, Oxford: Clarendon Press, 1995, p.199.
16. David M. Thompson, *Nonconformity in the Nineteenth Century,* Routledge and Kegan Paul, 1972, p.51f.

Chapter 2 — The Roots of Nonconformity

1. John Owen, *Works,* Banner of Truth, 1967, vol. 13, p.224.
2. Quoted, M. Watts, *The Dissenters,* Clarendon Press, Oxford, 1978, vol. 1, p.16.
3. Quoted, B. R. White, *The English Separatist Tradition,* Oxford University Press, 1971, p.12.
4. Ibid., p.11.
5. Ibid., p.15.
6. Ibid., p.16.
7. Patrick Collinson, *The Elizabethan Puritan Movement,* Jonathan Cape, London, 1967, p.88.
8. J. B. Black, *The Reign of Elizabeth, 1558-1603,* Oxford University Press, 1949, p.165.
9. Quoted, Watts, *Dissenters,* vol. 1, p.38.
10. Ernest A. Payne, *The Free Church Tradition in the Life of England,* SCM Press, London, 1944, p.34.
11. W. L. Lumpkin, *Baptist Confessions of Faith*, Judson Press, Valley Forge, 1969, 'Propositions and Conclusions', p.140.
12. *Mystery of Iniquity,* quoted, Watts, *Dissenters,* vol. 1, p.49.

13. Champlin Burrage, *Early English Dissenters,* vol. 1, Cambridge, 1912, p.287; Perry Miller, *Orthodoxy in Massachusetts,* Gloucester, Mass., 1967, pp.73-76; Geoffrey Nuttall, *Visible Saints,* Oxford, 1957, p.10; Watts, *Dissenters,* vol. 1, p.52.
14. Quoted, Joel R. Beeke, *Puritan Reformed Spirituality,* Reformation Heritage Books, Grand Rapids, 2004, p.129.
15. Quoted, John Morley, *Oliver Cromwell,* Macmillan, London, 1901, p.126.
16. Ibid., p.363.
17. Quoted, N. H. Keeble, *The Literary Culture of Nonconformity in Late Seventeenth-Century England,* Leicester University Press, 1987, p.33.
18. Quoted, Keeble, p.33.
19. Ibid., p.34.
20. Cited in C. Silvester Horne, *A Popular History of the Free Churches,* London, James Clarke & Co., 1903, p.174.
21. David Daniell, 'William Tyndale and the Making of the English Churches', *Tyndale Society Journal*, No. 9, April 1998, p.33.

Chapter 3 — The Nonconformist Minister

1. This essay has recently been republished in John W. Robbins, (ed), *The Church Effeminate,* Unicoi, The Trinity Foundation, 2001, pp.32-93.
2. All Scripture quotations in this chapter are taken from the British usage text of *The Holy Bible – New King James Version,* © Thomas Nelson, Inc., 1982.
3. This extract is taken from paragraph 3 of *the Savoy Declaration of the Institution of Churches and the Order appointed in them by Jesus Christ,* 1658.
4. The *Savoy Declaration,* paragraph 7.
5. There is some studied ambiguity on this point in the *Savoy Declaration* of 1658, but this has gone by the time you get to the Baptist Confession of 1677, published in 1689 as the *London Confession of Faith.*

6. 1 Cor. 15:8.

7. The *Savoy Declaration*, paragraph 11.

8. Benjamin Griffith, *A Short Treatise Concerning a True and Orderly Gospel Church*, 1743, 'Concerning Ministers, &c', section 3.

9. For example, Acts 8:17-19; 2 Tim. 1:6.

10. For example, Acts 19:11; 28:8.

11. Griffith, *A Short Treatise*, 'Concerning Ministers, &c', section 3.

12. The *Savoy Declaration*, opening paragraph.

13. Heb. 13:17.

14. 1 Peter 5:3.

15. 2 Cor. 1:24.

16. Gal. 2:11.

17. John Hooper (1495?-1555), formerly a Roman Catholic monk, became a Protestant and spent ten years in continental Europe before becoming the Anglican Bishop of Gloucester in 1549, and then of Worcester in 1552. A fervent supporter of the Reformation, he was particularly outspoken against the idea of ministers wearing vestments. He was burned alive during the Marian persecution.

18. Quoted by D. Martyn Lloyd-Jones, *1662-1962: From Puritanism to Nonconformity*, London, The Evangelical Library, 1962, p.12.

19. It is worth noting how very strongly this point is stressed in the 1689 *London Confession of Faith*, ch. 26 'Of the Church', par. 10.

20. Acts 20:28.

21. 1 Peter 5:2.

22. See 1 Tim. 4:15-16; 1 Peter 5:3.

23. See 1 Tim. 3:1-13, Titus 1:5-9, Acts 6:3.

24. James 3:1.

25. See John 10:11-13.

26. See Matt. 9:36-38.

Chapter 4 — Nonconformist Preaching

1. D. M. Lloyd-Jones, *Authentic Christianity: Sermons on the Acts of the Apostles*, vol. 1, Acts 1-3, Banner of Truth, Edinburgh, 1999, pp.306-307.
2. Bryntirion Press, 2005, pp.92-111.
3. Jay E. Adams, *Preaching with Purpose*, Presbyterian and Reformed Publishing Company, 1982, pp.52-53.
4. Hodder & Stoughton, 1971, p.98.
5. Brian Borgman, *My Heart For Thy Cause. Albert N. Martin's Theology of Preaching*, Mentor, 2002, pp.60-61.
6. D. M. Lloyd-Jones, *Preaching and Preachers* (Hodder and Stoughton, 1976), p.53.

Chapter 5 — The Decline of Nonconformity

1. D. W. Brogan, *The English People*, p.121, quoted in E. A. Payne, *The Free Church Tradition in the Life of England*, London 1944, p.121.
2. Michael R. Watts, *The Dissenters*, vol. 2, Oxford, 1995, pp.23-39.
3. James Munson, *The Nonconformists*, London 1991, p.117.
4. J. A. James, *An Earnest Ministry*, Edinburgh 1993.
5. Dale A. Johnson, *The Changing Shape of English Nonconformity*, New York and Oxford 1999, pp.62ff.
6. R. Tudur Jones, *Congregationalism in England 1662-1962*, London 1962, p.248.
7. Johnson, p.67.
8. Johnson, p.66.
9. Johnson, p.82.
10. Johnson, p.125.
11. Tudur Jones, p.259.
12. A. W. W. Dale, *The Life of R.W. Dale of Birmingham*, London 1898.
13. Johnson, p.174.

14. A. W. W. Dale, p.113.
15. R. W. Dale, *Fellowship with Christ*, London 1891, pp.263-264.
16. Johnson, p.180.
17. R. W. Dale, *The Living Christ and the Four Gospels*, London 1910.
18. A. W. W. Dale, p.312.
19. A. W. W. Dale, p.116.
20. T. H. Darlow, *William Robertson Nicoll, Life and* Letters (London 1925), p.365.
21. R. W. Dale, *The Atonement* (London 1902). See also H. D. MacDonald, *The Atonement of the Death of Christ* (Grand Rapids 1985), pp.242-249.
22. R. W. Dale, *Fellowship with Christ* (London 1891), pp.324ff.
23. Johnson, p.91.
24. Tudur Jones, p.174.
25. Johnson, p.89.
26. Tudur Jones, p.301.
27. R. W. Dale, pp.143ff.
28. J. M. Gordon, *Evangelical Spirituality from the Welseys to John Stot* (London, 1991), p.159.
29. R. W. Dale, *The Laws of Christ for Common Life* (London); *Week-Day Sermons* (London 1895).
30. Gordon, p.148.
31. Arthur Porritt, *John Henry Jowett* (London: Hodder & Stoughton 1924), p.226.

Chapter 6 — Nonconformist Anglicans?

1. David Mills, 'Collapsing Churches: A Sociological Analysis', *Touchstone*, 1995.
2. Robert Quinn, *Deep Change: Deep Vision* (Jossey Bass, 1998).

Chapter 7 — The Future of Nonconformity

1. J. I. Packer, *Among God's Giants: The Puritan Vision of the*

Christian Life, Kingsway, Eastbourne, 1991, pp.11-12.

2. T. Manton, *Works*, vol. 2, p.102f.

3. I. Shaw, *High Calvinists in Action*, Oxford University Press, 2001.

4. P. Lewis, *The Genius of Puritanism*, Carey Publications, Sussex, 1977, p.12.

5. Packer, *Among God's Giants,* pp.34-39.

6. Lewis, *Genius of Puritanism,* p.15.

7. Packer, *Among God's Giants,* p.42.

8. T. Watson, *A Body of Divinity*, Banner of Truth, Edinburgh, p.154.

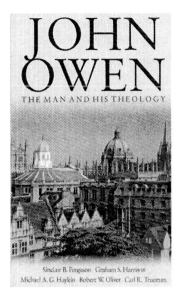

John Owen: The Man and His Theology

Edited by Robert W. Oliver

Evangelical Press
P&R Publishing Co.

ISBN-10: 085234502X

The chapters of this book were originally delivered as papers at a symposium on the life and teaching of John Owen at the John Owen Centre for Theological Study, London, England in September 2000.

John Owen's life from 1616 until 1683 spans one of the most momentous epochs in the history of Britain. How should we assess this man of so many talents, in turn a country pastor, an army chaplain, head of an Oxford college and vice-chancellor before becoming a leader among the persecuted Noncomformists? Beginning with an overview of his life and the times he lived in, the contributors to the symposium consider various aspects of John Owen's theology and the impact that his work had on his own day and ours. As Carl R. Trueman states in his paper, 'I do wish to commend Owen to students, ministers, and thoughtful Christians in general, as a good example of how theology can be done in a serious and profound manner.'

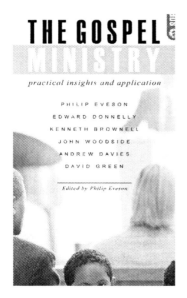

THE GOSPEL MINISTRY

practical insights and application

PHILIP EVESON
EDWARD DONNELLY
KENNETH BROWNELL
JOHN WOODSIDE
ANDREW DAVIES
DAVID GREEN

Edited by Philip Eveson

The Gospel Ministry:
Practical Insights and
Applications

Edited by Philip Eveson

Evangelical Press

ISBN-10: 085234595X

The chapters of this book were originally delivered as papers at a symposium on the gospel ministry in the present day at the John Owen Centre for Theological Study, London, England in September 2002.

Evangelist, pastor, teacher — today's gospel minister juggles several different roles. As Andrew A. Davies says in his paper, 'Pastoring the flock of God in today's world is a challenging business. This is partly because the pastoral office itself is under attack, partly because professionals have taken over pastoral functions, and partly because pastors have to deal with an often-bewildering variety of pastoral difficulties.' From the biblical foundations of gospel preaching through a historical review of pastoral ministry to a look at ministry in the context of contemporary society, the contributors to this book evaluate the work of gospel ministry, explore in detail the roles of pastor, teacher and evangelist, and conclude with an examination of ministerial training.

A wide range of Christian books is available from Evangelical Press. If you would like a free catalogue please write to us or contact us by e-mail. Alternatively, you can view the whole catalogue online at our website: www.evangelicalpress.org.

Evangelical Press
Faverdale North, Darlington, Co. Durham, DL3 0PH, England
e-mail: sales@evangelicalpress.org
Evangelical Press USA
P. O. Box 825, Webster, New York 14580, USA
e-mail: usa.sales@evangelicalpress.org

Printed in the United Kingdom
by Lightning Source UK Ltd.
125289UK00002B/88-498/A